THE ART OF HUTTING

THE ART OF HUTTING

LIVING OFF-GRID WITH
The Highland Hutter

Peter MacQueen

BLACK & WHITE PUBLISHING

First published in the UK in 2023 by
Black & White Publishing Ltd
Nautical House, 104 Commercial Street, Edinburgh, EH6 6NF

A division of Bonnier Books UK
4th Floor, Victoria House, Bloomsbury Square, London, WC1B 4DA
Owned by Bonnier Books
Sveavägen 56, Stockholm, Sweden

Copyright © Peter MacQueen 2023

All photography except for images listed on page 244 by Euan Anderson

All rights reserved.
No part of this publication may be reproduced,
stored or transmitted in any form by any means, electronic,
mechanical, photocopying or otherwise, without the
prior written permission of the publisher.

The right of Peter MacQueen to be identified as Author of this
work has been asserted by him in accordance with the
Copyright, Designs and Patents Act, 1988.

The publisher has made every reasonable effort to contact copyright holders of images. Any errors are inadvertent and anyone who for any reason has not been contacted is invited to write to the publisher so that a full acknowledgement can be made in subsequent editions of this work.

A CIP catalogue record for this book is available from the British Library.

ISBN: 978 1 78530 500 9

1 3 5 7 9 10 8 6 4 2

Layout by Black & White
Printed and bound in Latvia

www.blackandwhitepublishing.com

A Choinnich, 's ann an dèidh iomadh turas sona còmhla riut fhèin aig a' bhothaig, a bha sgrìobhadh an leabhar seo a' dèanamh ciall dhomh. Cha bhithinn airson a dhol ann còmhla ri duine sam bith eile fon ghrèin.

Tha gaol agam ort, Pàdruig

HUTS

Contents

01 Introduction

13 The Shielings

39 The MacQueen Hut

65 Meet the Hutters

93 Earth

119 Fire

145 Water

169 Huts About Scotland

191 There's No Place Like Your Hytte

215 The Hut Life Chose Me

235 Happy Hutting!
237 Glossary of Gaelic Terms
242 Ceud Mìle Taing – A Hundred Thousand Thanks
244 About the Author
244 Image Credits

Recipes & Hutter's Hacks

---

49 Hebridean Baker's Gingerbread Crumble
52 Useful Knots . . . Made Easy by Dad
59 Chaya's Masala Hot Chocolate
61 Katrina's Elderflower Grapefruit Gin Punch
83 Trish's Vegan Wild Garlic Pesto
113 Baked Strawberry Jam
114 The Zeer Pot
117 Hutter's Chutney
122 Devices for Your Stovetop
128 The Fiery Art of Lighting Your Stove
132 All About Foraging . . . For Kindling
134 The Perfect Outdoor Fire
139 How to Make Your Own Log Lanterns
141 Faye's Fired Aubergine Pasta
143 Pizza Dough
162 Birch Tapping for Beginners
167 Wee Rab's Hut Toddy
202 Nettle Soup
210 Pinecone Bird Feeder
228 Harnessing the Power of the Sun

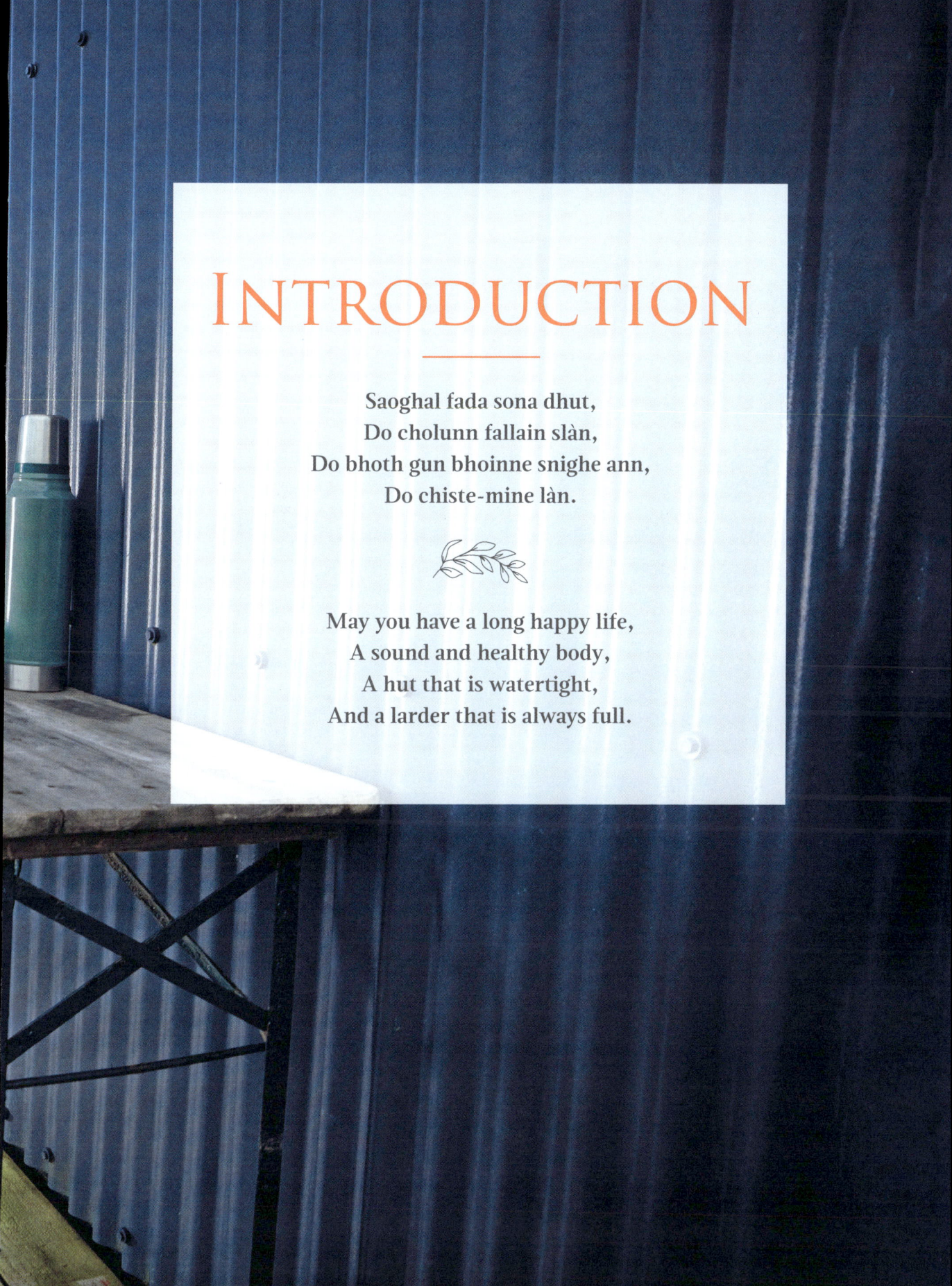

Introduction

Saoghal fada sona dhut,
Do cholunn fallain slàn,
Do bhoth gun bhoinne snighe ann,
Do chiste-mine làn.

May you have a long happy life,
A sound and healthy body,
A hut that is watertight,
And a larder that is always full.

Close your eyes and picture the perfect day at your own wee hut. What would it be like? Are you digging up your early potatoes, ready for the first taste of homegrown vegetables of the season? Or perhaps you're busy gathering, chopping and storing firewood to keep you warm through the winter months? Maybe you're around the table with friends, playing another round of gin rummy by candlelight with a dram in hand. Or simply sitting by the stove, in your favourite comfy chair with a dog or two snoring at your feet, as you enjoy some peace and quiet...

FÀILTE A CHÀIRDEAN, I'M PETER, THE HIGHLAND HUTTER.

If you have picked up *The Art of Hutting* and started to read, then I hope it is because you are drawn to the idea of a simpler life through hutting, which means we are kindred spirits. Perhaps you are already a hutter – and if so, then it is my wish that you find as much solace and inspiration in the pages that follow, as you do in your hut. If you dream of a hut of your own, welcome to what might be the first step towards making that dream a reality.

My goal with this book is to offer you a glimpse of the hutting lifestyle in Scotland today, introduce you to some of the amazingly resourceful and hospitable hutters I have met through my own hut life escapades and to give you some inspiration on how to embark on your own hutting journey. Plus, plenty of examples of what you might like to do in your hut once you've built it... although, of course, the possibilities are limitless!

A hut is what you make it. A hut is for holidays and day trips, weekends away, family time, friends time or simply you time. Hobby houses or even a taigh-cèilidh, they are a place to gather. Perhaps a place where you plant a garden and grow your own veg. A place to recharge the batteries in a world that puts so many demands on us. A hut is a sanctuary; it is a space that feels like your home away from home.

Visits to our wee bothag are incredibly precious to me and my partner Coinneach. Along with our dog, Seòras the Westie, we revel in the chance to head there whenever we can – eagerly anticipating the opportunity to disconnect and escape off-grid, to hang out together away from phones, emails and the stresses of everyday life. The minute our bags are unpacked, the fire is lit and the kettle is gently whistling on the stove top, we all start to relax.

One day in 2014, my father arrived back at the house with a van filled with windows that our neighbour was about to throw out. When we asked what on earth he was doing with them, he told us his plans: "I'm going to build a hut when I retire." And that is exactly what he did a few years later. After buying land on an inaccessible shoreline in Argyll, he began his journey. It wasn't an easy one, but, as broadcaster, journalist and author Lesley Riddoch observes in her amazing book, *Huts: A Place Beyond*, being eccentric helps if you want to surmount the challenges that present themselves to would-be hutters. And Lesley should know, for she has a PhD on the topic of hutting! You have to be pretty determined if you are going to build a hut, but it can be done. And my dad is certainly both eccentric and determined! If you're seeking inspiration, support and know-how, there exist many communities of huts – old and new – all populated by hutting individuals who will be happy to help guide you.

In Canada there are cabins, in Russia the *dacha*, in Scandinavian countries they are called *hytte* in Norway, *sommerhus* in Denmark and *stuge* in Sweden. Our Celtic nations have strong historical links with seasonal or informal buildings, too. In Scottish Gaelic a hut is called a *bothag*, in Irish Gaeilge the word is *bothán* and, similarly, in Welsh it is *bwthyn*. These three words most likely stem from the Old Norse *būð*, which also gives us the word *bothy* in Scots. The Scandinavian – in this case, Norwegian – influence

on the etymology around these traditional wee structures is interesting, especially as the culture of the *hytte* as a space away from home designated for recreation time is practised so strongly by our Northern European neighbours.

From a very young age, many of us appear to possess the seemingly innate urge to create a makeshift house to play in. After all, who hasn't hung blankets over chairs and made a wee hideaway in Granny's kitchen? Or used branches on a hillside to make believe it's a castle. Or dreamed of a storybook treehouse? In childhood, these spaces are simply called dens. The imagination of children shows us precisely what a hut is.

As it turns out, 2014 was a very special year for hutting in Scotland, and not only because my dad saved some old windows from landfill – windows with which he would eventually form a simple sanctuary for himself, my ma and our extended family – but also because the long-term work of many campaigners for the hutting cause, such as Reforesting Scotland, paid off. Following the Land Reform 2003 Act, much of the Scottish Government's planning framework and policies expressly supported low impact and sustainable activity, and clearly all aspects of the hutting movement have the potential to increase low carbon living. However, although we might think it's easy to articulate what a hut is, without a proper definition how could potential hutters

apply for planning? So, it was a historic moment when the Scottish Planning Policy definition of a hut was agreed as follows:

> **Hut –** *A simple building used intermittently as recreational accommodation (i.e. not a principal residence); having an internal floor area of no more than $30m^2$; constructed from low impact materials; generally not connected to mains water, electricity or sewerage; and built in such a way that it is removable with little or no trace at the end of its life. Huts may be built singly or in groups.*

Building a hut of your own is undoubtedly a challenge, but fortunately in Scotland we have an array of cabins, off-grid pods and huts to rent, all of which make getaways easy, adventurous and relatively affordable. They are a wonderful way to test if you have a hutter's heart. I have listed some in Chapter 9 – The Hut Life Chose Me (see page 221) for you to consider staying at, and you can easily find many more online.

What is clear is that at our latitude – from Canada to Norway and throughout Northern European countries where woodland terrain exists – cabin culture is the norm. My hope is that the art of hutting will continue to grow here in Scotland so that we can make it our normal too. After all, hutting is known to offer a substantial range of positive impacts on our physical and mental well-being.

These benefits are evident when you meet someone who has a hut. Just listening to them enthuse about the pleasure their wee bolthole gives them is delightful and astounding. Many describe their hut as having overtaken their home as the focal point for family life. A hut can enable a family members and their friends to strengthen and deepen connections with each other, with nature and the outdoors. Most hutters don't want to leave their hut at the end of their trips, and so the urge to return before too long is strong, thereby reinforcing positive and healthy lifestyles.

Are you feeling inspired? I hope so! Let's delve further into *The Art of Hutting*.

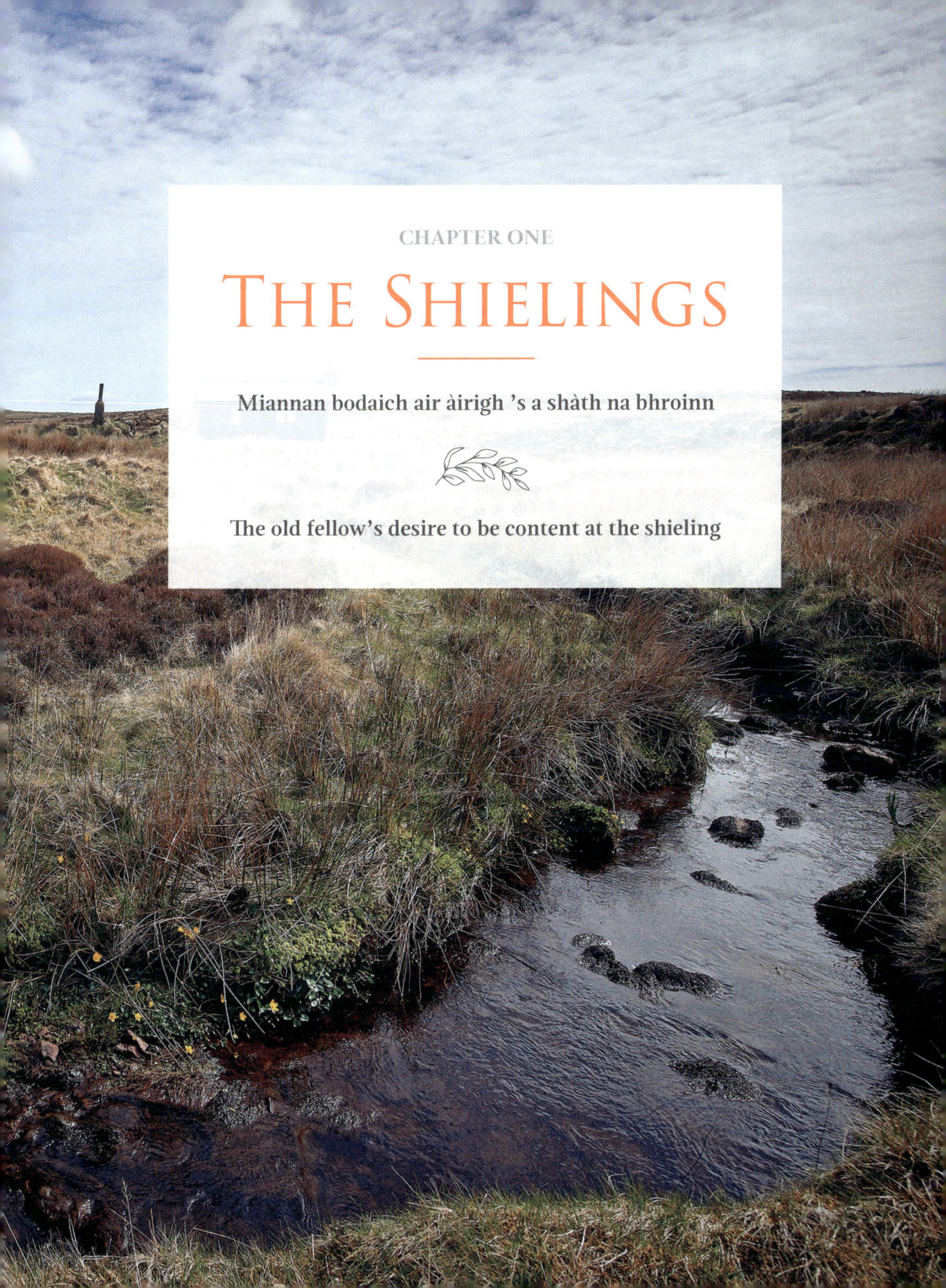

CHAPTER ONE

The Shielings

Miannan bodaich air àirigh 's a shàth na bhroinn

The old fellow's desire to be content at the shieling

Let's begin by examining the origins of informal buildings in Scotland. And where better to start than in the Western Isles with a visit to a site in the Isle of Lewis that remains close to its hutting traditions and history.

The drive to the shielings was long and bumpy, so I took my time on the rough moor road. I stopped to call the minister, to check that I was on the right track. He chuckled kindly at my alarm and assured me that I was. "Keep going, it's further than you think!" he said. "The kettle is on the stove – we'll have tea when you arrive."

Reassured, I trundled on. I passed a bodach with his old collie dog, cutting peats by the roadside. He waved to me, and I watched him disappearing in my rear-view mirror as he returned to his work with his tairsgeir, slicing lengths of dark peat from the bank and laying them out to dry. A flock of geese flew overhead in their perfect V formation, and I followed them in our shared direction.

I knew I had arrived at the àirigh (pronounced ah-ree) when I saw my friend, the Reverend Iain MacRitchie, at the side of the road. I pulled over and he shook my hand with a warm smile. "Fàilte, you made it!" he beamed. The wee huts that peppered the moor behind him looked cosy and welcoming.

Iain led the way through the heather towards his hut and, as we approached, I could smell the peat smoke in the air. "Come in and we'll make a copan," he told me, before adding yet more enticingly, "my sister has made a duff!"

We sat around the wee stove and chatted, while tucking into the tasty clootie dumpling. Our conversation meandered and I learned about the MacRitchie family connection to this part of the moors at the north end of Lewis. Like generations of Niseach families before, trips to the àirigh were a part of life: "I've been coming here to Cuidhsiadar since I was a baby," Iain explained. "Growing up in the 1980s, my brother, sister and I would walk out that road and visit our grandparents who had a caravan here... that was our summer holidays. I have loved it ever since."

The àirighean on Skigersta moor represent many eras. There remain some that are built with stone and have a turfed roof, in the style of a mini blackhouse. Others are a snug but ramshackle patchwork of corrugated iron, odd windows, offcuts of wood, felt and slate; that is, made with whatever materials their owners could readily access. There are a few whitewashed stone structures that mirror in miniature the white croft houses that became common in the island's villages from the 1920s onwards. I was pleased to see that there are also some newer builds, in a variety of contemporary styles.

"There is a real community and visiting all the àirighs around here as a child was very special. You knew the people who would come to each hut," Iain told me, remembering, too, how "we used to call in for a cèilidh wherever there was smoke coming from the chimney".

These happy early visits have clearly had an impact on Iain. After a stint of keeping a caravan here as an adult, he decided to build his own àirigh. "I always wanted a hut – so ten years ago I designed this one. I made a wee plan and then I got a local builder called Buckie to build it. We've never looked back."

Like all the hut owners I've met, Iain's face lights up as he talks about the building process. Creating a hut of your own is a necessary "life moment" that seems to rise up in certain individuals. The way they describe it, it is almost like it pushes its way to the top of their bucket list, leapfrogging all other hobbies and pastimes.

"The V lining previously adorned the walls in an old mission hall in Galson," said Iain, detailing the provenance of his hut's features. "The frayed carpet was in the manse dining room in Ness; the curtains were my great-aunt's and the chairs belonged to my granny and Shen . . . everything has a story, and it has all been repurposed here," he mused. "I find this to be a very spiritual place. There are no distractions here, so it is really good to come, recalibrate and get back to basics."

That perhaps encapsulates the idea of the àirighs; in their simplicity, they reflect another time and there is something rather appealing about that. They are also always evolving. Today they are primarily used for recreation, but in the past people built these structures with the purpose of shelter in mind. Although the shielings are thought of fondly in Gàidhealach culture, they were definitely places of work.

As we talked, Iain spotted smoke coming from the chimney of Àirigh a' Bhealaich and we decided to walk up the hill to visit Dòmhnall Ailein Mhòir (Donald, the son of big Allan), who had just arrived with his daughter Maggie. As we walked up, we waved to another couple – Màiri and Seonaidh – who were working outside their hut. "It can be smashing to come out here and see old friends," Iain said with a smile.

Donald was born in 1937 in the village of Lionel. Now that he is eighty-six, he has been coming out to this stretch of the moor – just a few miles from his family home – for over eighty years. Donald himself is a big friendly character who welcomed us into his hut to sit with him by the fire, while Maggie kindly offered us tea.

He has witnessed many changes to àirigh culture in his lifetime. He told me how his first memory was of cutting peats there with his great-grandmother, Seonaid, who was still visiting the àirigh in her nineties. In the 1940s, while his father was away at war, he remembers running over the moor after school to visit his grandmother, who would walk out there with the cow each May, where she would then stay for a few weeks.

It was to an original-style, stone-built àirigh with a turf roof that they would come. Donald told me how he and his granny would sleep at one end, with the cow at the other – which was a remarkable method of heating the hut – like a form of central heating, he added with a smile. There would be a wee fire on the floor in the centre of the hut, which his granny would cook on. His memories were of spending many long, happy days there throughout his childhood.

On the first day of the school holidays, he and his two sisters would walk out to the àirigh with their bags packed. When they arrived, they would run inside for a cup of milk and one of their granny's fresh scones. While the cows were on the moor, they would not have as much milk, but it would be richer – a taste Donald remembers fondly.

One of his favourite memories was the sight of long beams of sunlight coming into the dark hut during the day, through wee gaps in the turf. And, as for the night, he maintains that the sleep you get out at the àirigh is the best.

Now Donald's daughter Maggie comes out here for wee trips with her own family. Maisy Kate aged seven and Archie, who is nine, love it the same way their mum and Shennie do, and just like their great-great-great-granny Seonaid did too! A remarkable living link within one local family to a culture that was once commonplace throughout many parts of Scotland. Indeed, history shows that transhumance – a type of pastoralism or nomadism, which includes the seasonal movement of livestock between winter and summer pastures – was common practice in many places in Europe; thus, there is a rich folklore surrounding this seasonal activity.

I spent a wonderful day at the àirighean, and I left feeling humbled, inspired and grateful to Iain and the other members of the community for sharing their home, their stories and their history with me. I hope to return sometime soon.

IF THE STONES COULD SPEAK...

So, the vernacular history of Scotland is dotted around the countryside. Evidence of our connection with informal buildings is to be found often in wee ruins, and sometimes in modified versions of what once was. We live in a culture where the presence of little huts integrated with domestic housing was once the norm.

As my partner Coinneach is also Leòdhasach – a native Hebridean from the Isle of Lewis – we are frequently in the islands. Driving, or better still walking, around certain parts of Lewis offers us a window into those remnants of the culture that existed across Scotland for centuries – that of na h-àirighean or shielings. Perhaps you, too, have driven along the Pentland Road and seen a cluster of these wee buildings dotted along the roadside. Or the iconic, green-roofed shieling on the Barvas moor, opposite the famous hill named Muirneag. Along with the Cuidhsiadar àirighs, these are among the last of the surviving traditional shielings held by local families as part of their crofts – their connections with family, topography and the land itself much like those of the peat banks and common grazings.

The bothan-àirigh were constructed of local materials, such as stone and turf, or sometimes animal skins. And these simple structures with a single room and a fireplace were used for sleeping, cooking and storing food. People would not be idle while at the shieling; they would often spend their time making butter, cheese, knitting, loch fishing or mending nets, clothes or tools. The distance from home to àirigh would vary depending on local geography, but they could usually be reached within a few hours of walking. There would be frequent traffic between the village and the àirigh, with people walking back and forth to visit, deliver messages or return with fresh produce such as cheese or butter.

These links with the earth are captured in our comprehension of an àirigh. We understand it to mean not only the wee hut, but also the associated piece of land, which – as we have seen – would be visited during the summer months to graze animals. Traditionally in Scotland, the livestock would be cattle – as described by Dòmhnall Ailein Mhòir when he mentioned his grandmother walking out to her àirigh with her cow – but also sheep, goats or even ponies. The livestock were moved away from the nucleus village to let the main crops mature; this traditional practice was a vital component in how the seasons influenced patterns of life in these communities. This is reflected in many traditional songs about time spent at the shielings; very often they are love songs, which may allude to romantic encounters in the summer visits.

ÀIRIGH A' CHÙL-CHINN

'N àm èirigh na grèine, cur fàilt' air a' bheinn,
Bu bhòidheach an àirigh am bràighe Chùl-chinn,
Na h-uiseagan 's na smeòraich cho ceòlmhòr a' seinn
'S na flùran a b' àlainn lem fàilte ga inns'

Sèist
O mar a bha nuair a bha sinn òg,
A' mireadh air an àirigh le mànran 's ceòl.

Bha solas air an àirigh cha b' ann bhon a' ghrian
Bha ceòl ann an uair sin nach cuala mi riamh,
Bha solas anns a' ghràdh agus dàn anns gach fiamh,
Is ùr-dhealt' na h-òige cur fonn air an t-sliabh.

Nach fhaca tu na caistealan 's ann asta dhèanainn uaill,
'S e bothanan na h-àirigh làn bainne blàth nam buail'
Na miosraichean 's na copanan 's na cumanan 's na cuaich
'S na caileagan ag itealaich mar dhealan-dè mun cuairt.

Sibh-se tha cho fiosarach am Pàrlamaid na tìr',
Thoiribh dhuinn na h-àirighean na mullaichean 's na frìth
Is thèid mi fhèin an urras dhuibh mar dhuine 's fhaide chì;
Gun dannsadh sinn 's gun seinneadh sinn "Gu ma fada beò an Rìgh"

Sèist mu dheireadh
Dìreach mar a bha nuair a bha sinn òg
A' mireadh air an àirigh le mànran 's ceòl.

THE CULCHINN SHIELING

At sunrise a welcome to the mountain.
Most beautiful was the shieling on the slope of Culchinn;
The larks and the thrushes singing so sweetly,
The most beautiful flowers, their fragrance testifying to their presence.

Chorus
O how we were, when we were young;
Frolicking in the shieling with crooning and music.

There was light on the shieling and not from the sun;
There was such music there then, that I've never heard it's like;
There was light in the love and poetry in every look,
And the fresh dew of youth adding to the beauty of every hillside.

Did you not see the castles, of them I would be proud,
The shieling bothies full of fresh milk from the folds,
The wooden dishes and cups, milking pails and bowls,
And the lassies cavorting like butterflies around.

You who are experienced in the country's Parliament,
Give us the shielings, the summits and the wild moorland
And I guarantee you, as one who is foreseeing,
That we would dance and sing "Long live the King."

Final chorus
Just as it was when we were young
Frolicking in the shieling with crooning and music.

ABOUT THE BÀRD

Iain MacLeod was born in the Highlands in the mid nineteenth century. The son of a crofter, he grew up to have a career in education, mostly in England, although he returned home to Assynt later in his life. He was well thought of in the community and affectionately known as am Proifeasair – the Professor. As you can see in this song, the bàrd speaks with great fondness of the shieling of his youth – even appealing to the powers that be to give the àirighean, the hills and the moors to the people. An insightful idea that was in some ways ahead of its time, it is echoed by many in modern Scotland in an era when community buyouts and land reform are still such a hot topic.

MOUNTAIN BOTHIES

Modern-day bothy culture echoes this past phenomenon of traffic of visitors seeking shelter and a place of comfort for the night. Indeed, it is Scotland's open network of bothies that facilitates many hill walkers' expeditions to the furthest, most isolated reaches of our wilderness. These bothies, unique in their unbookable, open-door nature are often maintained by the Mountain Bothies Association – the bulk of administration and maintenance is carried out by volunteers, which is funded by membership subscriptions and donations.

Think of bothying as camping without a tent; all your comforts need to be carried to the bothy, and all your rubbish carried out. Usually, there are no services such as running water, toilets or electricity, yet the craic we experience in bothies offers a perfect example of Scottish hospitality; they are places where weary walkers dry their socks, socialise and rest often around a warming fire fuelled by what they could carry in. Hearts and spirits are lifted as stories of the day are exchanged with generosity and camaraderie.

Learn more about Scotland's bothies, the Bothy Code and how to get involved via their website.
www.mountainbothies.org.uk

THE RUINS OF ÀIRIGH CULTURE

Whenever Coinneach and I are at his home village of Cromore in the Isle of Lewis, we enjoy walks out with our westie Seòras to some of the tobhtags – the ruins of àirighs. We find them fascinating. Although they are falling down and the walls are not more than a few stones high, you can often still make out where the entrance was situated. In other parts of the island there are still some beehive-style stone and turf examples of àirighs, which offer a glimpse of a more complete structure.

> **The Germanic etymology of the word "shieling" comes from *schele* or shale in the Northern dialect of Middle English, and is most likely related to Old Norse *skjol* meaning "shelter" and *skali* meaning "hut". The Gaelic word *àirigh* looks to be Celtic in origin; in Old Irish the word *áirge* seems to have been borrowed into Northern European languages – for example, the Faroese word is *ærgi*. This etymological story resonates with the historic movement of people between Scandinavian countries, Scotland, Iceland, Ireland and the Faroe Islands.**

I always find myself imagining what village life was like when they were in use. These walks are through dramatic scenery, and we will often pour tea from a flask at the site of an old àirigh as we pause and think about the people who might have walked here before us. Sadly, those times have now slipped from the living memory of the local people in Cromore, where Coinneach grew up. For me, this emphasises just how special it was to meet the community at Cuidhsiadar – but I appreciate, too, how through the songs of that era, and the ruins within the landscape, we glimpse the old ways. If only those stones could speak!

TRADITIONS

On Là Buidhe Bealtainn, or May Day – the first day of summer for the Gaels – a variety of different traditions were once observed. People would wash their faces in the dew for luck, cailleachs would make crosses out of fallen rowan tree twigs tied with wool to ward off bad spirits, cattle would be walked between two fires for protection, and people would decamp to the shielings with their livestock.

It is gratifying to witness the relatively recent resurgence of hutting in Scotland. This is largely thanks to the efforts of a small group of campaigners – indeed, as we have seen, my father was able to build his own hut as a direct result of their work in ensuring a definition of "hut" for planning regulations. However, the tradition of hutting is almost as old as the hills themselves.

TOBAR AN DUALCHAIS / KIST O RICHES

Although memories of the shieling's original purpose might be largely consigned to the past, resources such as Tobar an Dualchais enable us to explore archives of audio recordings of Scotland's folklore in Gaelic, Scots and English. Searching for shieling or àirigh – or indeed almost any topic that piques your interest – will open a door to a treasure trove of stories, songs and first-hand accounts. And, once you step inside, you can't help but become immersed in the crackly recordings of earnest voices telling tales of times gone by.

www.tobarandualchais.co.uk
Instagram @tobar_an_dualchais

THE SHIELING PROJECT

And if such voices inspire you to learn some of the crafts they would have practised, then perhaps the Shieling Project is for you. Here, you can experience craft holidays in the Scottish Highlands in an off-grid learning centre while staying in their huts – either at their site near Beauly, or at the one near Helmsdale. The project is all about the skills of outdoor living – from looking after livestock to the construction of buildings to the weaving of baskets. You can help with seasonal tasks like planting, haymaking and harvesting crops. You could try, too, a wide range of artisanal crafts such as carding, spinning or felting with wool from the project's sheep.

The traditional patterns of the shieling, where folk lived outdoors all summer, give us an insight into the past, but they also – through this type of increasingly popular tourism based on authentic cultural experiences – offer a forward-looking view to a sustainable future. Could such an experience become your gateway to the hutting lifestyle?

www.theshielingproject.org
Instagram @theshielingproject

AN ISLAND BOTHY

And as for Lewis? Well, I am delighted that there are new shielings being built in the present day. As we have seen, official recognition is vital to the continued evolution of the àirigh and Comhairle nan Eilean Siar – the Western Isles council – is supportive of planning applications for new huts to be used for recreational purposes in certain areas.

I met with one family in Uig to learn of their experience of building such informal structures. In particular, the awe-inspiring Mangersta Bothy, which John and Lorna Norgrove built with stone and wood over thirty years ago on the cliffs in Uig. It is a structure so integrated into its landscape that only the sunken squares of windows reveal its presence in the irregular layers of stone that form its rounded shape.

When the Norgroves were building their bothy, no one seemed too interested, nor did others perceive any value in it. However, over the years it has attained a near-legendary status of its own, and now people come from far and wide to experience this remarkable stone shelter.

The bothy can accommodate up to three people, but since it is not connected to any services, visitors should come prepared. Given its stunning location and extraordinary ambience, there is a high demand from spring to autumn and so bookings are usually restricted to one night.

It remains free of charge to stay at the Mangersta Bothy, but donations are welcome to the Linda Norgrove Foundation– a trust which gives grants to support women in Afghanistan. The Foundation was set up by John, Lorna and their daughter Sophie after their daughter, and sister, Linda Norgrove, was kidnapped in Kunar Province, Afghanistan, on 26 September 2010 and later died in an attempted rescue by US forces

on 8 October of the same year. She was thirty-six. Linda devoted her working life to helping others, and so she is not defined by the tragic circumstances of her death, but by the life she lived and the choices she made.

THE LINDA NORGROVE FOUNDATION

When the Norgroves were building the Mangersta Bothy, they found the cliff-top location so inspiring that they decided to work with the available material – which was mainly stone. They made the rocky roof at Mangersta incredibly strong, creating little fibreglass legs and using stainless steel wire to hold some of the stones in place. Much of the other materials were driftwood, recycled fence posts or pallets, all of which helped to keep the costs down.

In its natural materials, the bothy is very reminiscent of the stone hut on Sula Sgeir – the remote and uninhabited rocky island some forty nautical miles to the north of Lewis. The island is still frequented annually by the men of Ness, who have a licence to continue the traditional hunt for the guga, that is, the young gannets. Or the St Kilda huts on Stac an Àrmainn – where, remarkably, there is a bothy and around eighty cleitean, the stone structures used by St Kildans to store eggs and seabirds as a source of food, prior to the evacuation on 29 August 1930.

However you choose to approach it, building a hut is a very personal, creative process. The decisions you make will depend on your skill set, your location and what you are hoping to use your newly created space for. This last is a question that gives food for thought: what final result do you dream of? How do you envisage spending your time in your hut? One thing is for certain – places like the àirighs of Lewis, or the unique Mangersta Bothy are here to inspire a breathtaking range of possibilities. Without doubt, it was the presence of existing huts in their various forms that energised my own family into those actions that made hutting a cornerstone of our world. And we have never looked back!

www.lindanorgrovefoundation.org/mangersta-bothy

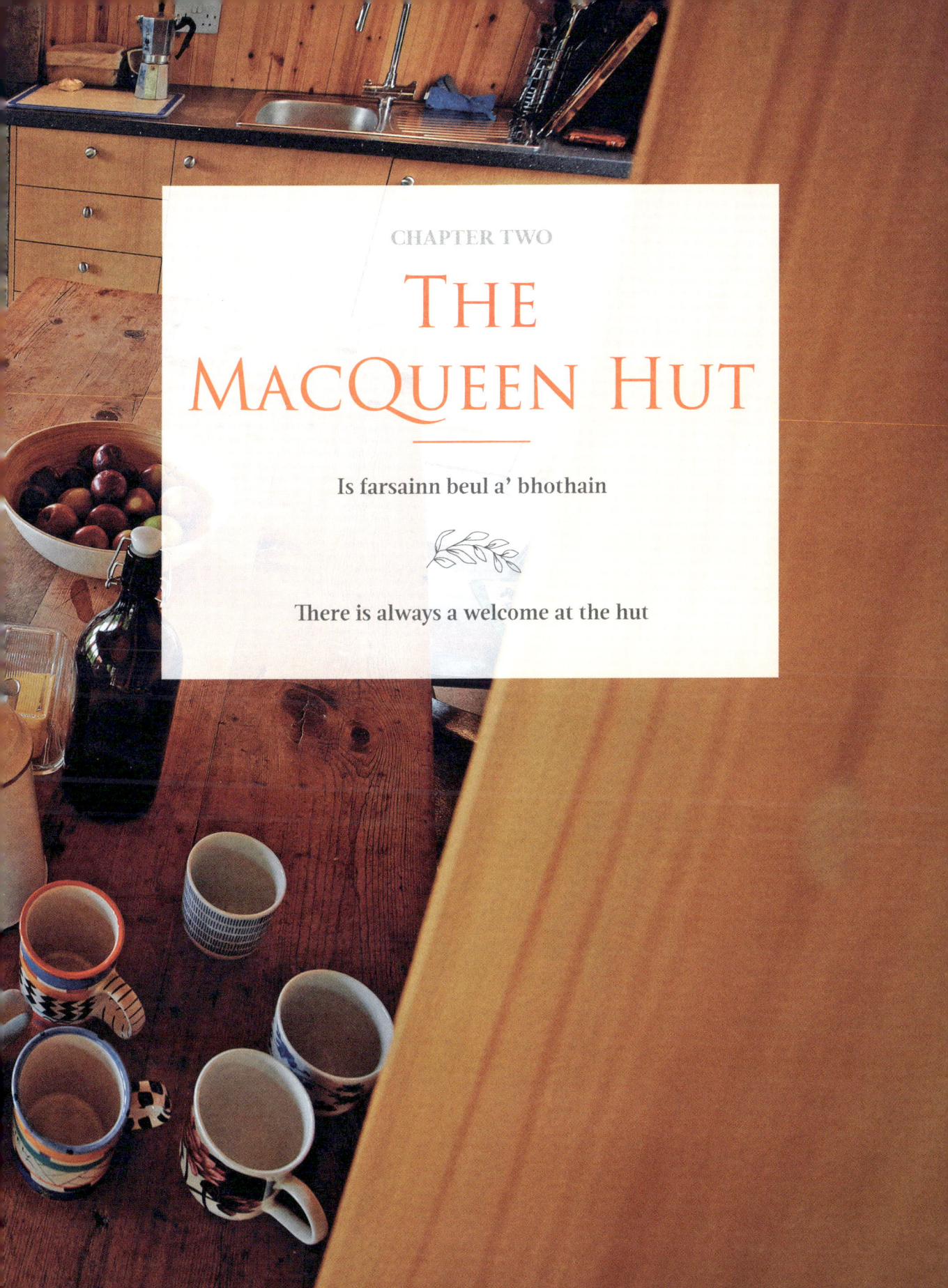

CHAPTER TWO

THE MACQUEEN HUT

Is farsainn beul a' bhothain

There is always a welcome at the hut

Hutting can be a conduit for change. And I hope it could be for you too ... I might be biased, but by my reckoning, the difference the hutting lifestyle makes to family life is entirely positive, and it is one that I've observed among many of the hutters I have met to date.

In Scotland, many of our activities are guided by the embrace of nature and the ebb and flow of the seasons. The summer gifts us with long, sunlit days, while winter bestows upon us even longer, dark, often cold and wet nights. Huts facilitate our connection with the countryside in a manner that more temporary camping experiences fail to provide. The act – and art – of constructing a humble shelter, a cosy haven to rest, relax, cook and slumber in, allows individuals to forge a profound bond between themselves and their wee bit hill and glen. The significance of huts extends beyond personal links, too, as wider familial ties and friendships are strengthened within these cherished spaces.

I was born in the late 1970s and grew up in Argyll in the 1980s – and I feel privileged to be a Gen Xer. We were the last generation to grow up before the rise of multiple TV channels, mobile phones and the internet. My brothers and I – along with our friends from neighbouring houses – would entertain ourselves by going out to play, where we would explore the hills and glens near our home, always returning at the end of the day with grazed knees, pockets full of treasures and stories to tell. We climbed trees, gathered brambles, went fishing in the loch and skimmed stones. We built dens prolifically – and expertly, too – everywhere we went, whether up in the branches of an old oak, beside a tumbling stream or to offer shelter in the hills!

When it was time for dinner, our mother would summon us back to base with a trusty whistle. Comically named the *Acme Thunderer*, its echo would ring out across the glen as we shouted "Coming!" and sprinted home for tea.

We were lucky to live in both the analogue and digital worlds. We knew what it was like to play outside all day, utterly free and without a care in the world, but we also knew how to use technology to stay connected with friends and family. But still, even though we can access the entire world with a few taps on a screen, there's nothing quite like building a den with your pals.

I find it comforting to realise that my childhood shared so many similarities with those of my own parents and, indeed, grandparents. Like me, they grazed knees and climbed trees – and, of course, built dens. Surely these experiences were a driving factor in my father's eagerness to build his hut – an idea born of his sense of play.

A ROOF AND A SEA FOR THE WORLD

In April 2017, that idea took further steps towards fruition when a local landowner agreed to sell my dad a parcel of land in a deal that really kickstarted our family's hutting escapades. The land is a former industrial site, situated at the entrance to Clachan Sound at the northern end of the Isle of Seil. It was once the Glen Albyn slate quarry, which was abandoned in 1905 when twenty-five men were laid off as it was deemed no longer commercially viable. The slate industry had been a major source of employment in the area for centuries and those men mined the very same seam of slate which runs through Seil, Easdale Island, Luing and Belnahua – collectively known as the islands that roofed

the world. I have a very fond memory of visiting the site with Dad shortly after the sale was completed. He was like a big kid, full of exuberance and energy; so excited at the possibilities ahead.

My father had chosen this site for two reasons. The first being that as a family we would often visit the shore there when out fishing for mackerel. The sea is in our blood. Dad's first training for a life sailing the seven seas had been playing in boats with his brothers in front of their house on Clachan Sound in the 1960s. He then became a merchant seaman, rising through the ranks and gaining his Master's certificate when he was only twenty-eight years old. His grandfather was Duncan MacQueen, a boatbuilder on Easdale Island and his other seanair was Coll MacFarlane, who operated the ferry between Seil and Luing, and had the croft at Cuan. My dad, just as his forefathers before him, knows the waters around the inner isles of Lorn even better than the back of his hand.

On my childhood fishing trips, my seanair would expertly row us gently up and down the sound in a boat called *The Jean*. My brothers and I would try to calm our excitement when the tug of fish biting on the hand lines that trailed behind the boat alerted us that it was time to tug back and haul a catch. If I caught any fish, I would always want to put them back in the sea and Uncle Stuart would shout, "No, we'll put them in the deep freeze." I sense that neither of us were particularly keen on the killing and eating part! When we got hungry, we would pull the boat up the shore – to just below where our hut is now – a fire would be lit to make tea and Granny would produce sandwiches and buttered gingerbread, much to everyone's delight, especially Uncle Stuart's, who is always up for picnics. I don't know why, but tea made on an open fire in the outdoors always tastes better.

The second, more practical reason that Dad wanted to build at Glen Albyn, was accessibility. While the ebb and flow of the tides present a challenge for boats entering the sound, the vast accumulation of weathered slate spoil from the old quarry, weighing in the hundreds of thousands of tonnes, has naturally formed the perfect landing spot. It is one that he realised would cater to my mother's needs and allow her to land in a place where she can manoeuvre her wheelchair with ease – a rare opportunity along the jagged coastline and a happy accident of the area's industrial past.

In May 2017, my dad started to clear the site. He would make regular trips in his boat, bringing the materials to build his wee hut in stages – often helped by Duncan MacEachan, who operates the ferry from Kerrera to Oban. They would wait for high tides, so Duncan's barge could bring prebuilt segments of the hut and land them on the shore in the same slated landing spot where my mother now comes ashore. This was a happy time for my dad, and he enlisted help from friends and family to assemble the building – a process which was eventually completed in summer 2018.

In the building of the hut, Dad expressed his creative, practical and loving personality. Not only did he use those windows destined for landfill, but what I find most remarkable is how he made it possible for my lovely mum to visit this wild part of Argyll.

The difference these trips make to her life cannot be overstated, but without the hut's careful situation it simply isn't a journey a lady in a wheelchair could make. But now they enjoy frequent visits, comfortable overnight stays and can host friends and family there for meals cooked on the stove. Truly life changing in every way.

In building this family space away from the home, my father has created a place that is both companionable and neutral. It has become somewhere where many family members and friends seek their peace and freedom.

QUALITY TIME

A hut, by definition, is a humble abode, built with love and an element of dogged determination, ideally located within an hour or two of travel from your home. The hut is the "other place" where you and your family or friends can go at any time for peace, release and sense of fellowship. However small the hut may be, its power and potential should not be underestimated. It holds within its walls a world of possibilities.

Beyond providing a refuge, the outside spaces of the hut offer an opportunity to cultivate a connection with the earth, to discover the joys of new growth and of witnessing nature unfold. They can become gateways to a garden, where vibrant flowers bloom and vegetables thrive under the hutter's nurturing green-fingered care.

Or the hut can be a painter's retreat, where every brushstroke dances across the canvas, bringing imagination to expressive life. Or the hut might transform into a writer's den, where words flow effortlessly, creating captivating stories or giving poetic voice to memories. Huts make particularly good havens for musicians, where melodies fill the air and dreams become song – and, of course, who doesn't love a cèilidh? In the solitude of their huts, the hutter seeks the freedom to explore their creativity and pursue their passions.

HEBRIDEAN BAKER'S GINGERBREAD CRUMBLE

SERVES 8

We are truly spoiled by Coinneach's baking prowess – I take my role as the Hebridean Baker's cake taster very seriously! It is a tough job, but someone has to do it, right? This crumble is autumn in a bowl and if your hut doesn't have an oven, then it is one that can be prepared at home and then heated on the stove top at your hut. Using two different apples gives a combination of textures that works perfectly with the warmth of the ginger. Topped with an oaty crumble, the only thing left for you to do is smother it in custard.

INGREDIENTS

For the filling
- 5 cooking apples, e.g. Bramley
- 2 eating apples, e.g. Braeburn
- ½ tsp ground ginger
- ½ tsp mixed spice
- 125g demerara sugar
- 1 lemon, zested and juiced
- 6 stem ginger balls in syrup

For the topping
- 200g unsalted butter, chilled and cubed
- 250g plain flour
- 50g demerara sugar
- 50g flaked almonds
- 50g jumbo rolled oats
- 75g ginger biscuits

METHOD

Preheat the oven to 180°C (fan).

Peel and slice your apples into large chunks, chop up the stem ginger and combine all the filling ingredients together in a bowl before adding to a 1½ litre oven dish.

To make the topping, rub the butter into the flour in a bowl until the mixture resembles breadcrumbs. Add in the sugar, almonds and oats. Finally crush the ginger biscuits into the crumbs, then stir in and then scatter evenly over the apples to cover.

Bake for 45 minutes or until the topping is golden and the fruit filling is bubbling at the edges. Serve with custard.

FAMILY TIES

A hut is not limited to solitary pursuits. It may serve as a common ground for families and friends, a place where memories are etched into the collective consciousness of kinship. Parents and children, uncles with nieces and nephews, cousins with their kids, lovers and friends – all the wonderful variations of human connection – gather around the hearth of a wee stove, sharing laughter, food, wisdom and stories. A hut is a space where generations intertwine, strengthening the bonds between young and old. The hut becomes a vessel for new traditions, a place where the rich diversity of ties among family and friends are nurtured and celebrated.

Huts also offer a bridge to the wider world. They can become a meeting point for like-minded souls, a gathering place for community. Here, individuals find kindred spirits who share their love for nature and the simple joys of life. Huts become remarkable hubs, where friendships are forged and shared experiences form the foundation of lasting relationships.

In the MacQueen family, our hut means my mum can enjoy time in the great outdoors with all her boys; my brother Mark likes to go there and pick up the fishing rods with his pals; Uncle Stuart loves to declare the view "beautiful", his arms outstretched in praise of the vista! Dad visits to potter with friends and works hard at the hut's upkeep. For him, as carer to Mum and Stuart, it represents a vital source of respite.

Myself, I like to potter and make time for hobbies, and I especially enjoy taking the time to plant things and tend the garden while Coinneach bakes at the stove. My nephew Ruaraidh and niece Abby have loved toasting marshmallows in the fire since they were wee; their heights are etched on the wall in pencil – proving, in time-honoured tradition, just how much they've grown since the hut came about. But who loves the hut most of all? Well, my money's on the dog! Of us all, Seòras really knows how to live in the moment – and commandeer the space in front of the fire. Visualising us all like this, I can't quite believe how much history our family and our friends have created around this wee structure – and I look forward to making many more happy memories there as the future unfurls before us.

HUTTER'S HACK

USEFUL KNOTS . . . MADE EASY BY DAD

Whatever your choice of outdoor pursuit – hiking, sailing, paddling, climbing or pottering in the garden – knot-tying is an essential skill that takes hours of careful practice to master. There are thousands of different knots for an almost infinite number of uses, but here we focus on three invaluable knots for hutters. These are Bowline, Sheet Bend and the Timber Hitch – a trio which are easy to learn and simple to tie and untie.

1. BOWLINE

This knot is used to form a fixed loop in a piece of rope. It is easy to untie even after being put under strain.

1. Make a loop in the rope.

2. Pass the end of the rope (the "rabbit") up through the hole.

3. Then round the back of the "tree".

4. And back down the hole again.

5. Pull the knot tight.

6. Sometimes the bowline is called the "king of knots"!

2. SHEET BEND

This knot is used to tie two different pieces of rope of varying thickness together.

1. Make a loop.

2. Take the second piece of rope, then pass it through the loop.

3. Take it around the back and pass it under itself.

4. Tug tight and the two are joined.

3. TIMBER HITCH

This knot is used to attach a rope to a cylindrical object or objects. It's good for towing logs or carrying bundles of branches for the fire.

TOP TIP! If you want to make sure you can tie your knots correctly in all conditions or eventualities, then my dad says you should practise tying them blindfolded! Aye aye, Captain MacQueen!

1. Wrap the rope around the pile of wood (or whatever it is that you want to bind).

2. Pass the tail of the rope around itself.

3. Then wrap it through the gap.

4. Do this three times.

5. Pull it tight.

6. Lift your load, and off you go!

CHAYA'S MASALA HOT CHOCOLATE

SERVES 2

I met Chaya at a Spanish language school in Argentina when we were both young and free spirited. Every day, after class, she used to say to me, "Let's go and do our homework at the pub." Of course, we never did any work, but ordering "Dos cervezas, por favor!" is surely an important life skill and we have been best pals ever since.

Our travels together now are always to the hut. For a London girl who feels the cold, holidays in Scotland can be hit or miss weather-wise, so Chaya is usually to be found wrapped up in a woolly geansaidh, coorie-ed in close to the stove with a warm drink in hand.

Chaya tells me that when she was a little girl, she was always given the job of making tea for Diwali visitors – and she is still very much the kettle queen! This recipe makes two generous mugs of hot chocolate and is inspired by her early brewing skills. The perfect way to warm up!

INGREDIENTS

500ml milk
50g dark chocolate, 70%
2 cinnamon sticks
2 star anise
8 cloves
6 green cardamom pods
½ tsp nutmeg freshly grated
½ tsp ginger powder
Sugar, to taste
Pinch of paprika

METHOD

Put everything in a pan and heat very gently. In about 10 minutes it will be ready. Pass the hot chocolate through a sieve, and serve immediately. The warming blend of masala spices combines with the richness of the dark chocolate to create such a treat – it wraps round your heart like velvet. Gracias, Chaya – te amo mucho!

KATRINA'S ELDERFLOWER GRAPEFRUIT GIN PUNCH

SERVES 12

Elder is a remarkable shrub. It grows throughout Scotland, has a multitude of uses and seems to grow best when it has a bit of support from other trees, or a fence. You can forage for these wonderfully aromatic and sweet flowers from May to June, which is when they are in season.

Elder (English common name)
Sambucus nigra (Latin)
Droman (Scottish Gaelic)

The clusters of elderflowers are easy to harvest whole. But please don't strip the tree of all the flowerheads; leave some so you can go back for elderberries in the autumn, and remember to leave enough for the birds too. Never wash the flowers, as you will remove much of the fragrance – so be sure to check for insects before use. Bugs will not look so appealing suspended in drinks!

In the past, Highlanders believed the leaves of the elder to be effective in curing wounds, and they would attach elder sprigs to doors and windows to protect against bad witches' charms. Even now, elder berries make an excellent flu remedy, and once you're feeling better the flowers can be tossed in batter and fried as a delicious fritter.

My friend Katrina is a Shetlander and is always to be found at the centre of any cèilidh, so when she takes the bar into her own hands like a true Viking, she dispatches me and her wee boy Sonny to go gather elderflowers to flavour the drink. This punch recipe is a surefire winner whenever a group of pals get together at the hut.

TO MAKE TRADITIONAL ELDERFLOWER SYRUP

INGREDIENTS

750ml water
1kg sugar
1 lemon
10 elderflower heads
25g citric acid

METHOD

Boil the water, remove from the heat and add the sugar, stirring to dissolve fully. Grate the rind of the lemon into the pan, slice the lemon and add this along with the flowerheads and the citric acid. Leave for 24 hours, but stir it occasionally. Strain through a muslin cloth, then pour into a sterilised bottle. Your elderflower syrup should keep for six months.

TO MAKE THE PUNCH

INGREDIENTS

300ml Harris Gin
600ml apple juice
150ml elderflower syrup
1,200ml prosecco
2 pink grapefruits, juiced
Cucumber rounds, thinly sliced to garnish
Apple rounds, thinly sliced to garnish
Ice, for cooling (if available)

METHOD

Add all the ingredients to a bowl, swirl to mix the flavours. Then, if you have ice, add some to keep your punch cool. Slàinte mhath and skol, Katrina!

A TIME AND A PLACE FOR EVERYTHING

Ultimately, a hut equates to more than simply owning a physical structure. It is an invitation to integrate hutting into one's very way of life. It means embracing the simplicity and serenity – the realness – that huts offer and making them a part of your routine. It is about finding joy in life's little moments, about nurturing links between yourself and others and the world around you, and it is about immersion in the beauty of nature.

Across the Scottish countryside, the wee huts that dot the landscape stand as testament to the incredible possibilities that lie within their humble walls. In a country as small as Scotland, with its relatively low population, I truly believe there should be room for huts for everyone – so that we can all unlock these good times. Time at the hut, is time well spent – however you wish to spend it!

If we look to the experiences of hutters throughout the land, the eclectic, positive effects of this lifestyle are clear. This shines through in the words of our old songs about visits to the àirighs, where the bàrds fondly recount the visits to remote grazings by ordinary village people. Or the trend of post-wartime hut builds by working-class families close to Scotland's industrialised urban centres. Looking back in history, we see that hutting was the pursuit of all kinds of working people looking for a little bit of fun. Let's go; it's time to meet some folk from the hutting community...

CHAPTER THREE

Meet the Hutters

Druididh gach eun ri ealtainn

Birds of a feather, will hut together

It's always a privilege to travel to new places in Scotland, but it has been an added delight for the purpose of those travels to be to visit, meet and experience such a diverse range of huts, hutters and hut sites. I can't help but notice how, throughout the country, clusters of new huts have emerged, while also being aware that there are long-standing examples that have adapted to the changing times, while preserving their own rich histories and distinct characters. Here are a few stories from historic huts and the hutting friends I made on my hutting tour of Scotland.

GAMES LOUP – SOUTH AYRSHIRE COAST

I first met my friend John at a party in a flat in Glasgow. It was November 2000, the cocktails were flowing and we were all fresh-faced and just out of uni. Daft Punk was playing on the CD player; their new single "One More Time" was the song of the moment. With French electronica as a striking soundtrack for our conversation, I remember being intrigued as John talked passionately about something I'd never heard of before. Huts.

John's family own a clutch of neighbouring huts in a stunning seaside location, overlooking the tiny granite island of Ailsa Craig. When John was growing up, there was Granny and Grampa Cowie in the central hut, then John's great-auntie Joyce and her husband Bert next door to them. Uncle David had his hut up the hill and John's parents had the hut behind Granny. They really are true hutters. Hut life for them is a family affair!

Communal holidays and weekend trips formed the basis of family life throughout John's childhood. "We should all go and visit there one weekend," he enthused, as Daft Punk was put on repeat. It is close to comical that, nearly twenty-five years later, I found myself finally taking him up on the invitation. Aptly enough, I'm listening to *Discovery* – singing along and chair dancing, thinking about how music has *got me feeling so free...* – as I drive down the M77 to the Ayrshire coast to meet his parents, Jackie and David.

They were busy outside their immaculate hut when we arrived. The garden is so tidy and well kept, a sure sign that they make regular visits. I knew Jackie was John's mum the minute I saw her; they are like two peas in a pod. I felt at home immediately as I sat down to tea and biscuits with this lovely, friendly couple and Jackie started to tell me stories about Games Loup.

Jackie's family have roots going way back in this bonnie part of the Ayrshire coast. In the 1840s, her great-granny's family lived in Carleton Fishery. She was called Agnes McCreath Thompson and would come home with her family from Govan for holidays; this later became a family tradition – one that was made possible by huts.

Much later, during the Second World War, Jackie's dad, Bill Cowie, and his siblings were evacuated to Carleton Fishery. They then continued to holiday there after the war, camping at first. She remembers her very first holiday to Games Loup – they stayed in a converted bus. The Cowie family would spend the whole of July there, with her dad visiting on weekends after work and staying for the Glasgow Fair. This family didn't go "doon the water"; they went doon to the hut!

There were no facilities then: it was gas stoves, candles, Tilley lamps and a wee wash in the burn. The best drinking water came from the Whisky Well – a freshwater spring that was up on the hill. The water was so clean, so cold and so delicious that Auntie Maggie would ration it so there was enough for all the huts.

Jackie and her brothers Norman and David loved playing on the beach all day. Sometimes they would pick whelks on the shore, and then potatoes from the field where the caravan park is now, after the howkers – the pickers employed by the farmer – had left. She is

not sure exactly when, but eventually huts were built at Games Loup – about ten in total – all with families like them who would come for wee trips and holidays. Auntie Maggie would rent her cottage and then move into her hut next door for the summer. Jackie remembers these summers as a lovely, worry-free time, with all the family rubbing along contentedly together with communal meals, lively parties and the kids running feral and free.

If only we could go back in time to ask the post-war hut builders what exactly motivated them. Perhaps their huts were a response to the enclosed, pressurised atmosphere of urban life and an expression of the human need to get out into wilderness spaces. Or were they simply using some of the skills acquired via increasing industrialisation and the trades commonly practised by Clydeside working-class people – such as joinery, ship fitting and plumbing. Whatever the initial impetus, it seems that when one hut was put up, more were sure to follow. Perhaps that post-war era was the golden age of hutting – in a time when there was renewed hope of a better future for everyone and just before cheap flights, increased car ownership and package holidays became a reality.

As I look around the Games Loup huts, I smile to myself and remember John back at the party in Glasgow, rhapsodising about his passion for hutting. Here, now, and I can see why – this must have been a magical place to spend time as a kid. The close positioning of the huts, with a close-knit family unit regularly descending on them, knowing that the time ahead would be spent playing on the shore, hearing the old family stories again and enjoying each other's company and the location. Then, as if she can read my thoughts, Jackie tells me how happy she is that her own sons, John and his brother Andrew, had the same opportunity to share and enjoy these holiday experiences, as she did. "There is something very comforting about that," she muses. While the experiences have a quality of timelessness about them, as the years go by, the huts themselves are modernised and upgraded. Even hutting must move with the times if it is to survive and thrive.

In 1984, it was discovered that the A77 above the Games Loup huts was unstable. The authorities wanted to divert the road back to the Old Coach Road along the shore and over the top of their wee bit of hutting paradise. The hutters had to fight to prevent this.

An action group was formed, and eventually they succeeded in keeping many of the huts safe, although some families were not as fortunate and in 1988 the three huts closest to the road were demolished. Jackie explained that this action meant they lost neighbours whom they had known and called friends for many happy years. As part of these works, the spring was also covered up and that was when mains water was installed.

But now, the Games Loup huts are safe as they move into the care of the next generation of hutters on the sunny Ayrshire coast: John and his brother Andrew now have Uncle David's hut, and when Auntie Joyce passed away her family took that over. I can't wait to visit again. In fact, John, next time you are at the hut give me a shout! Daft Punk have hung up their helmets, but hutting continues and, naturally, *we're gonna celebrate…*

THE CARBETH COMMUNITY – STIRLINGSHIRE

I first visited Carbeth in 2018, around the time my father was finishing his hut build. I wanted to visit the community there and see huts that had – for an entire century – stood the test of time. So, I drove out past the Milngavie reservoirs of Craigmaddie and Mugdock – examples of Victorian engineering at its best. These reservoirs are home to a commemoration stone honouring John F. Bateman, the mastermind behind the project. They play a crucial role in his rather intricate water system, which was completed in 1860. This system spans a distance of 41.5 kilometres north to Loch Katrine and connects to the Greater Glasgow area through a further 13 kilometre aqueduct consisting of twin cast-iron pipes that descend southward to the city. Thus, Bateman made clever use of gravity to transport water and improved sanitation to the "Weegies" of the nineteenth century and beyond. But, as I drive past, my thoughts are not of the downward flow of water surging through the pipes, they are of the first hutters – men and women who relied on muscle power and sheer resourcefulness to lug materials up here to build their huts.

Nestled in this woody nook of Stirlingshire, nine kilometres to the north of Clydebank, lies Carbeth. This site, with its 177 huts, is steeped in history and cherished by generations. Since its beginnings as a popular camping spot in the pre-war years, Carbeth has evolved into Scotland's oldest, most beloved traditional hutting community, enchanting families from Glasgow and the Clydeside area.

Carbeth's tale is one of resilience; it is a place born from altruism and forged through adversity. In the aftermath of the First World War, when returning soldiers yearned for solace and fresh relationships with nature, landowner Allan Barns-Graham granted them the right to camp on his land. At first resisted, his act of humanity would lay the foundation for a community of hutters.

WILLIAM FERRIS: PIONEER

At the heart of this story stands a remarkable man named William Ferris, who hailed from Govan in Glasgow. Born in 1894, Ferris embodied a pioneering spirit that would shape outdoor access for Scottish people. Ferris's involvement in the movements that created opportunity for Scots to access the great outdoors is nothing short of amazing. Having served in the Highland Light Infantry during the First World War, he came back home with a vision: to bring the healing power of fresh air, tranquillity and access to Scotland's more rural landscapes to working-class families along the industrialised River Clyde.

Inspired by the Scottish countryside, determined and emboldened by his experience of war, Ferris employed his talents as a skilled communicator and penned a heartfelt letter to Allan Barns-Graham, beseeching him for permission to build a humble hut at Carbeth. The landowner turned him down, but offered camping rights instead. An unusual rapport blossomed between the unlikely duo, which eventually led to the birth of the Carbeth hutting community. The condition laid down by Barns-Graham was that Ferris would collect the rents and organise the hutters – which he did from 1920 to 1943.

Ironically, as the Carbeth huts grew in number, Ferris didn't have a chance to take one for himself owing to his commitments with such a breadth of organisations and committees, including the Camping Club of Great Britain and Ireland, the Scottish Council of Physical Recreation, the Scottish Rights of Way Society and the Federation of Ramblers – and many more to boot! He was even involved in the establishment of the Scottish Tourist Board and Glasgow's Citizens Theatre. However – and despite the myriad regulations limiting the activities of Carbeth hutters in the early days – Ferris's enduring efforts enabled many families to start their hutting journey as part of the expanding community at Carbeth. Access afforded by huts with rules appended was better than no access at all. And so it would be fair to say that Ferris and those first hutters instigated the modern hutting movement.

Over the course of its remarkable 105-year history, Carbeth has weathered storms both literal and metaphorical. The community has faced challenges, such as unjust rental hikes, evictions, insecurity and even mysterious fires that have reduced a few huts to ashes. But, through it all, the spirit of Carbeth has prevailed – a testament to the strength, perseverance and camaraderie of its residents. In a landmark moment of triumph – following many struggles, spanning decades, that culminated in a rent strike – the land was transferred to community ownership in 2013, ensuring the preservation of Carbeth's legacy for generations to come. As I'm sure William Ferris himself would agree, surely there's no one better to oversee the future of Carbeth, than the Carbeth hutters themselves.

OUT AND ABOUT IN CARBETH

Explore the community on foot and you'll encounter an intriguing blend of hut styles, encompassing vintage and contemporary designs – with everything in between. The huts – ranging from ramshackle to extravagant – offer up pleasing variations in appearance; some might be adorned in the classic green colour, while others showcase a more modern aesthetic. The assortment of solar panels, weathered glass doors, reclaimed timber, along with an array of extensions, sheds, outbuildings and neatly stacked woodpiles, creates a captivating diversity. This remarkable community really does serve as a one-of-a-kind springboard for aspiring hutters everywhere.

CARBETH CHARACTERS

ALLAN AND ELIZABETH both grew up visiting family huts in Carbeth... Though the sprawling size of this hutting site – or perhaps it was fate? – kept them from crossing paths as children. Allan's family hut sat by the tranquil loch, while Liz's stood proudly on the other side of a big hill. However, their destinies intertwined one night at the Carbeth Inn when Cupid's arrow struck the young couple, leading to a Carbeth wedding!

Now, Allan and Liz relish time spent in their cherished hut, not only as a couple but also as parents and foster-parents. Their hut has hosted around one hundred different kids over the years – and thanks to the energy of this good-hearted couple, many youngsters have experienced the positive effects of hut life. Their humble deck, extending gracefully outside their hut, has become a renowned gathering spot for evening socials. Laughter and conversation fill the air as friends and family soak up the atmosphere. As a member of the Carbeth committee – who has dedicated countless hours to guiding and nurturing the community's spirit – Allan's unwavering commitment to the principles of hutting shines through.

SARAH, a vibrant soul bursting with creative energy, expresses her artistic passion through the creation of organic-inspired sculptures. A talented artist, she finds solace and inspiration in the Carbeth community garden, where she tends to its plants alongside her wee helpers, grandchildren Rowan and Meadow.

ALI AND NEIL, stalwarts of the community, proudly keep their old-school hut overlooking the loch, amid a tapestry of mature trees. Their classic Carbeth hut exudes a sense of charm and nostalgia; its expansive window frames the lochside vista and seamlessly merges the beauty of the outdoors with their welcoming abode. Ali is a gregarious character who delights in hosting the ladies' singing group at their hut. She knows just how good singing is for the soul – of individuals and of the community.

TRISH is a very green-fingered hutter who finds solace in her woodland haven. Her cosy hut, snuggled in a leafy spot, is not only her sanctuary but also a welcoming home for her two beloved dogs Jazz and Kelsey, and a mischievous cat called Luna. With a deep appreciation of nature, Trish adorns her garden with wildlife cameras, capturing brilliant imagery of birds nesting, playful rabbits hopping, deer picking their graceful way past, and foxes traversing the midnight landscape. Her garden's tranquillity is matched only by its productivity, in her cultivation of a bountiful array of vegetables. For those seeking a taste of her foraging expertise, here is Trish's recipe for Vegan Wild Garlic Pesto – a delicious delight for the senses in early spring!

TRISH'S VEGAN WILD GARLIC PESTO

I visited Trish's hut on a beautiful spring day when the sun was shining through the trees, casting dancing shadows on the ground. Trish's well-kept garden boasts a vegetable patch and a variety of trees and shrubs. That day, she was particularly proud of her new addition: a wild garlic patch. Planted last year, it was now spreading naturally –and Trish was happy to report that the deer had not yet eaten any of the wild garlic; an added bonus!

Wild garlic is a very fragrant herb that has long been popular in Scotland. It comes up in the spring, just as the hunger gap is beginning to yawn. At this time of year stores are low, but the garden has yet to yield useful crops. Foraging wild garlic is easy: it smells, as you might expect, garlicky! The broad leaves grow in clusters, and the attractive white flowers grow in a star shape and form little spheres. You can harvest both the leaves and the flowers.

We picked some, being careful not to damage the bulbs at the roots, so the plants will return again next year. We then took the wild garlic back to Trish's hut, where she showed me how to prepare it. She made a truly flavoursome vegan wild garlic pesto, which we ate with pasta. Try it for yourself; I doubt you'll find a more mouth-watering way to enjoy these fresh springtime herbs.

INGREDIENTS

40g wild garlic
½ lemon, juice and grated zest
50g hazelnuts
50g pine nuts
50g vegan Parmesan, grated
Glug of extra virgin olive oil
Pinch of salt and pepper

METHOD

Freshly pick your wild garlic leaves and rinse them in water, then dab dry in a clean teacloth. Crush them in a pestle and mortar with a pinch of salt, then add both types of nuts to the paste and continue. Add the olive oil, grated cheese and lemon zest, along with a twist of the juice – and keep pounding. When you have the texture you like – smooth or chunky – you can stop!

This pesto is delicious in pasta, in salad, on toast or in sandwiches. You can store it in a jar by topping with some olive oil; it will keep in the fridge for a few weeks.

EDDLESTON – SCOTTISH BORDERS

As I strolled down the slope among the leafy assortment of huts in Eddleston, the sound of conversation reached my ears. Intrigued, I followed the voices, guided by the laughter coming from one of the wee huts.

I found Moo and Stwie sitting on their deck – mugs of tea in hand – enjoying the evening light. They invited to me join them, immediately poured me a cuppa and started to tell me about their hut life. This is one of my favourite things about hutters – they are a sociable tribe and unfailingly welcoming to newcomers. Muriel's family are part of the history of this farm field full of huts in Eddleston; she has been coming here since childhood. And their hut is home to many of Moo's memories – as a self-proclaimed collector, lots of sentimental objects decorate the space. Stwie, on the other hand, is a practical force. He takes me on a tour to showcase the newly fitted door, demonstrate the inner workings of the solar panel invertor charger and to proudly present the vibrant wall mosaic he crafted using colourful pieces of pallet wood.

Together, they love to improve and develop the hut, but it's a constant work in progress. Stwie compares having a hut to the Forth Rail Bridge in terms of maintenance; no sooner have you finished but it's time to start at the beginning again – you're always to be found paintbrush in hand! Eager to share their passion for their hut, hanging out with them feels easy and natural. As I am about to leave, Moo says, "Sure you won't have another cuppa?" I decline with a heavy heart; truly, they are a breath of fresh air and I could have stayed there blethering all night. But fear not: I'll be back to that deck for more hutting havers soon.

SOONHOPE GLEN – PEEBLES, SCOTTISH BORDERS

As I followed the burn through the huts and up the glen at Soonhope, birds chirped tunefully, and sunlight dappled through the leafy canopy overhead. I could see the Parker family on the deck outside their hut and a chuckle escaped me as I recalled my recent phone chat with Dougie, where he referred to his family as being like "The Broons going to the But 'n Ben".

I crossed the footbridge and was making my way along the path towards them when I was met by a mischievous pair – a boy and a girl armed with water pistols! The wee girl skooshed me and then they both ran up to the hut, their shrieks of laughter echoing behind them.

I pulled up a pew at the table and was introduced to the whole clan – believe me, there are lots of them. "This isn't even all of us," Dougie announced with a smile. "Pour the man a cup of tea." I was then introduced to the matriarch of this hutting dynasty – their very own Maw Broon – Janet, who is affectionately known as Jinty. "I see you met my great-granddaughter," she said, pointing at my wet shoulder. "Yes," I replied with a grin, spotting how Maiwen and Freddie were still sizing me up, pistols at the ready.

The family are from Motherwell, but Jinty, who is eighty-six, tells me that her granny was from Peebles and she is how the link with Soonhope first began. She explains that the original hut in the glen was owned by a Musselburgh family, who used it for holidays and weekends. Then the next lot of three huts were occupied by a retired gamekeeper and two brothers from Peebles, who had fallen on hard times.

When Jinty was a wee girl in the 1940s, many of her family were hutters. There was Jeanie – Aunt Jean – who was her dad's eldest sister, James Dow, Ella, Uncle Davie, the Bruntons, and all their families, plus her own mam and dad and of course "aw the weans". Her dad's sister, Auntie Jenny and her husband Uncle Bill had seven sons and a daughter. Jinty grins at me, her eyes dancing with merriment, as she asks, "Can you imagine trying to squash them all in a wee hut?"

Jinty tells me how the farm owners never minded the hutters being there; indeed, she remembers old Bob Jackson – clad in his tunic-style long shirt – nodding to them as they walked past. She laughs as she recalls an incident involving the hen hut, which was situated up the glen. Her cousin plotted to sneak in and pinch some eggs, but was foiled upon finding that once his head and ears were through the hen-sized entrance he was stuck. There was only one way to free him: the "grown-ups" had to saw around his lugs! He never attempted to swipe an egg again.

As kids, they didn't grasp how fortunate they were to have the huts as a childhood escape from town life. Jinty remembers how they delighted in these and other countryside escapades, such as the time she had to chase after an escaped pig, while her family watched in fits of laughter. "I have never been on a horse," she says, "but I did ride a cow at the huts once!"

Jinty describes the struggle of carrying luggage to the hut – to cross the burn into the glen you either stepped along two railway sleepers or waded through the cold water – which meant those who owned cars were looked upon with serious envy. However, the lack of a vehicle didn't dampen their spirits too much – and it certainly never stopped them from coming. As more huts were built, the valley became busier and eventually a bridge was constructed at the point where water crossed the dirt track route in. "Glory days," exclaimed Jinty. "Dry feet!"

During the early years at the hut, paraffin lamps, primus stoves and candles were used for cooking and lighting. Then lights and a cooker fuelled by Calor gas were installed. Striking a match became a magical shortcut, eliminating the laborious tasks required for making even a simple cup of tea. And, by that time, they had added an extension to the back of the hut, dividing it into two small bedrooms, making it all feel quite posh.

Over the years, other significant changes occurred. Solar panels were installed, providing lights at the press of a button. Heavy quilts and blankets were replaced by duvets – another example of the difference made by modern amenities, Jinty marvels. Still, the simple pleasure of flying her kite was her favourite pastime at the hut, though she admits that onlookers might have found it odd: the sight of a young mother flying a kite.

Many of the new hut owners are unaware of the challenges faced by hutters when the council decided to formalise ownership in the 1970s. Before they were allowed to stay, each owner had to hire a surveyor to ensure their hut met the legal requirements and building regulations. Huts formed of old buses had to be removed within a year, and railway carriages had a three-year deadline, although one defiant carriage remains to this day.

Soonhope Glen residents claim to have glimpsed renowned personalities in their midst. Legends abound of sightings of Princess Margaret, Ava Gardner, and Oliver Reed – who frequented The Crown. He even had a dedicated seat in this local pub, affectionately dubbed "Ollie's chair".

As the community grew, and huts appeared on the upper slopes adjacent to the road, the glen became a bustling hub of activity. Binmen, ice cream vans, bakers and mobile shops would all drive up to the huts, prompting the kids to ask for a penny to buy a lolly!

To hear this family's stories about these huts is such a pleasure. I hope that one day in the future when Maiwen and Freddie are, in turn, grandparents sitting on a deck outside their huts, they will regale the younger generation with tales of adventures here with their great-granny and all the family too!

CARRY ON HUTTING

Our forebears built the traditional hutting sites of Scotland with resilience and hardiness – sometimes against the odds, too – acquiring materials, transporting them to suitable sites and then making the time to build. If that is a challenge today, it surely was an even tougher challenge then. They would be proud to know that huts remaining today have endured. Now, they are frequented by those who have often continued hutting in the face of adversity – further evidence, perhaps, that hutting is good for us. Why else would those fortunate enough to have a hut persevere with their love of hutting if it were not lots of fun and good for body and mind? The individuals who have preserved these early huts and the sites they exist on really have paved the way for modern hutting – and we salute them!

CHAPTER FOUR

EARTH

Biadh a thoirt don fhearann mus tig an t-acras air,
Fois a thoirt dha mus fàs e sgìth,
A ghart-ghlanadh mus fàs e salach,
Comharran an deagh thuathanaich.

To feed the land before it gets hungry
To give it rest before it grows weary
To weed it well before it gets choked
Are the marks of a good farmer.

Your hut can be the perfect spot to grow a garden, plant an orchard, cultivate a vegetable patch – or it can just be a place to feel grounded. The culture of recreational hut use has the potential to bring people closer to nature and to restore practical skills – which have perhaps been lost between the generations – such as growing food, caring for a garden or planting trees. Fostering that interaction between people and the earth is essential to the hutting ethos; seemingly small, individual actions taken by hutters can and really do contribute to a transition to a low carbon world.

ALL ABOUT SOIL

Soil is a mainstay of life on planet Earth. It is the habitat of billions of species in our diverse ecosystem, from micro-organisms up all the way through the food chain.

When soil is healthy, it provides nutrients that feed our plants, trees and crops; it is part of the natural cycles that filter the world's water supplies. It protects against flooding and helps combat drought; its self-sustaining cycle can regenerate. The bad news is that we have lost half of the Earth's topsoil in the last hundred and fifty years owing to intensive farming practices, which contribute to the significant decline in soil health. This could pose a major threat to food security in the future.

Acting as a natural medium for carbon capture and storage, soil helps to balance the impact of climate change. In fact, there's more carbon held in the soil than there is in all the plants, forests and in the atmosphere combined. Locally, nationally and globally, it is essential to our existence. We need to preserve and conserve soil and we can help to do this by taking meaningful action as individuals. Our actions can make a real difference, and so here are three suggestions for what hutters might usefully do.

1. GROW YOUR OWN VEGETABLES

Your very own hut veg patch is an environmentally friendly and inexpensive way to grow your own food – and help recycle nutrients back into the soil. You can share any excess produce with your friends and family and contribute a little to other local food networks. The difference in taste, too, makes it all worthwhile: homegrown is always best!

2. MAKE A COMPOST HEAP

Organic matter from your kitchen scraps, fallen leaves and grass clippings is an essential ingredient in healthy soil, helping it maintain water and nutrients. You can add your compost to your soil, and this will give it a huge boost!

You can save buying a special plastic bin by building a compost box out of old pallets. Lining it with old carpets on the base, sides and lid will help heat the pile and aid the transition from waste to your own homemade, organic compost.

TOP TIP! Citrus in the compost heap tends to take much longer to decompose. Chop it up into small pieces to assist the break down.

3. PLANT TREES

Another way of aiding the soil at your hut is to plant trees, and if you choose to plant fruiting trees you will of course get to enjoy their crop. Trees are deep-rooting and they can help prevent compaction, while promoting healthy soil structure and drawing nutrients from deeper in the soil for use by other plants.

We planted Victoria plum trees, plus a mixture of apple and pear varieties at our hut. They are now starting to bear fruit every year, which is ideal for homemade pies and puddings – luckily, we have a Hebridean Baker in the family! Apples store well for a few weeks in a cool, dark place. Plums, pears and apples can also be easily frozen for use throughout the year. If your friends are anything like ours, they will be glad of the gift of fresh fruit for their kitchen. Oh, and did I mention... homegrown is always best!

However big or small your orchard, planning is key to its success. Be sure to check the size of rootstock your bud stock has been grafted onto, as this will indicate how large you can expect trees to grow.

ROOTSTOCK GUIDE

M9	For a small tree, approx. 2.5m tall.
M26	For espaliers and cordons.
M27	For trees in pots.
MM111	For trees up to 4 metres tall.
M25	For large standard trees, approx. 4 to 5 metres tall.

TOP TIP! Do your research to see which varieties will suit the style and size of your orchard. Fruit-growing success depends on two things:

1. Choose the right varieties for your location.
2. Plant them with enough space for their predicted growth.

Investigate which old heritage varieties have grown well near where you are, as chances are they will grow nicely for you. Seek the advice of nearby gardeners. For us, in Argyll, we have found that apple varieties such as Allington Pippin, Baker's Delicious and Coul Blush have thrived. More mainstream favourites to try might be Katy, Devil's Blush and Bramley.

If you are looking for fruit trees in Scotland, check out **www.scottishfruittrees.com** for expert help and a broad range of varieties.

Nurturing our garden and making the *Gàrradh Phàdruig (Peter's Garden)* BBC Alba programmes has been one of the greatest pleasures of my life. Spending time with Coinneach, and Seòras, in the gardens at home and at the hut has been rewarding in ways that I never imagined. It feels so good for body, mind and soul – and don't forget that learning as you grow is all part of the process.

MY THREE TOP TIPS ARE:
1. Don't be afraid to fail – every gardener knows you win some and you lose some.
2. Harvest and eat – or store or give away – produce that looks ready.
3. Try not to get carried away with buying too many seeds – focus on a few plants to begin with.

LOW MAINTENANCE OPTIONS

Gardening and hutting go hand in hand, but as most hutters visit intermittently – at the weekends and holidays – it is wise to consider low maintenance options that can still give you that lovely rush of green fingered satisfaction. However, you can plan your activity in line with the frequency of your visits. My dad, for example, visits his hut many times a week for day trips – so a wee veg patch works well for us as the bodach can check things over, keep on top of the weeding and get the watering can out when needed!

If your visits are not so frequent, perhaps you could plant trees that will provide you with nuts, such as walnut or hazel? Or soft fruits? A thicket of raspberries, lingonberry, gooseberry, redcurrants, brambles or a wee strawberry patch will do particularly well and can thrive even when left to their own devices – especially if you cover them with a net. After all, as you will notice as you explore Scotland, we have wild varieties of many of these fruits which take care of themselves.

SIX MORE IDEAS TO GET YOUR GROWING PROJECT UNDERWAY

RHUBARB – iconic in crumbles and, once established, it comes back year on year under its own steam.

RADISHES – brilliant for kids to grow as they are easy, and quick to harvest; you can also eat the young leaves in a salad.

LETTUCE – fast and fun to harvest as and when you need it in true pick-and-come-again style!

BULBS, BUSHES AND FLOWERING PERENNIALS are another way to satisfy the urge to grow. Why not take a trip to your local garden centre and see what takes your fancy? If you are not sure which plants to buy, I recommend a visit during the summer months and simply select the plants that sing to you. That way you get an instant splash of colour at your hut, one which you know will return year on year.

Daffodil bulbs are easy to plant and create a knockout splash of springtime yellows, whites and oranges. Duncan and Kate at Croft 16 specialise in selling a stunning range of daffodil bulbs, mostly antique varieties bred before 1930. I love to browse their catalogue and buy vintage Narcissus cultivars, giving myself a pat on the back at the same time because I'm helping ensure their survival. Always try to support small specialist nurseries when you can.

www.croft16daffodils.co.uk

A wildflower meadow might be your passion, as it will encourage bees, wildlife and biodiversity with minimum fuss. In which case, check out Scotia Seeds for their wildflower seed packets and meadow mixes.

www.scotiaseeds.co.uk

GROW YOUR OWN VEGETABLE PATCH

Vegetables need decent soil, plenty of sunlight and regular water to grow. When we plant vegetables at the hut, we usually work seaweed into the soil in the winter. It works wonders as a fertiliser – by the time we come to plant in spring, it will have rotted down and enriched the soil. If you don't have access to the seashore, then perhaps you can source manure.

In your first year of growing, don't fall into the classic trap of trying to do too much. This is a mistake that many people growing their own veg for the first time make. I know I did! I would recommend starting with just a few veggies, preferably ones you really like to eat. That way you will have more time to look after those few different items, and you will find yourself learning with them as they grow...

Once you've chosen what you want to grow, sow your seeds inside and transplant them out when the last frosts have passed. This will give your seedlings chance to be stronger ahead of the growing season as it begins in Scotland. Timing is crucial as those tricky late frosts through April and May can catch you out. The old wisdom that urges, *Dinna cast a cloot till May is oot* goes for seedlings too!

And so, our windowsills are full of pots and trays with seeds through February and March. A trick I learned from my granny and seanair, who were brilliant home

gardeners, is to put any containers that are not germinating into the airing cupboard. This regulates the temperature, and the seedlings should then pop through. Next, you simply move them to the window for light.

Even tasks such as weeding that might feel mundane at home can become a pleasant experience if you are visiting your hut. I like to check how the veggies are progressing and pull out any little weeds as I go.

Gardeners love to share their hard-earned knowledge and can be an incredible source of shared passion and understanding. Don't be shy about asking them for tips and advice! Either in person, or you can read books, magazines and online articles – including the seed packets, which often feature plenty of useful information.

So, if you are starting out with home vegetable growing, then keep it simple at first. If you are already accustomed to growing, then why not have fun and play? Either way, four wee beds which you can rotate year on year is a nice clean way of organising your patch, but you could begin with just one bed and introduce more later as your confidence and expertise grow.

Sadly, Scotland does not have a vegetable seed producer; the closest geographically is Real Seeds in Pembrokeshire, West Wales. We always buy from them via their website; they have been producing a variety of really good heirloom and modern seeds for over twenty years and we think they have a beautiful company ethos.

www.realseeds.co.uk

BED 1 – *Potatoes*

Growing your own potatoes is a brilliant experience, and you really will appreciate the difference in texture and taste. Source your seed potatoes locally if you can. You will find that most places have an allotment society or a gardening club that will arrange a seed sale early in the year. My favourite varieties are Golden Wonder, but I have also grown Epicure, Red Duke of Yorks and Maris Piper with success.

Potatoes like a rich soil, so it is worth digging in some compost and seaweed if you can get it in the winter, as this will improve the soil ahead of planting in the spring.

The first part of the process is to place seed potatoes in the window for a few weeks to sprout – this is called chitting. Then, planting them on St Patrick's Day is always good practice. When the potato plants pop through the ground, seasoned growers like to hill the earth up around them – this trick will help the plant yield more tatties. Harvest your potatoes when the flowers are past and the green shucks are dying back.

BED 2 – *Brassicas*

Cabbages, broccoli, cauliflower and kale are easy to grow, but I advise putting a 3mm-diameter net over them to keep off the birds and the butterflies.

One of my favourites to grow is calabrese. It is much more tender than shop-bought broccoli and the plants produce one main head, which after harvest then produces smaller side-shoot florets – so you get to enjoy another harvest from them.

When you choose where you are going to plant them, make sure no other brassicas were planted there the year before. This helps to keep the soil healthy and is why it is good to rotate beds if you can. Brassicas like a rich soil, so dig in plenty of organic matter such as well-rotted manure before you intend to plant.

If you can, sow from seed at home and bring on the little plants yourself, ready to transplant into the ground after the last frost. Especially in Scotland, this will help give your plant a head start and will offer greater yields at harvest time. In twelve to fourteen weeks' time you should be ready to eat fresh calabrese for your dinner, but the young tender leaves can also be eaten like cabbage.

BED 3 – *Root vegetables*

Radishes, beets and turnips are strong contenders for the root vegetables bed, but my favourite in this category is carrots. Carrots come in a variety of shapes and colours. Why not try a purple variety for fun? You need the soil to be as stone free as possible for the long roots to grow straight. If you don't have space to plant them in the ground, they also grow well in buckets.

Sow your carrot seeds directly into drills about 2cm deep and 15cm apart. Keep the soil damp and be patient; they can be slow to germinate. It is a good idea to weed regularly to remove unwanted neighbours when the carrots are young, so as not to disturb the crop later.

Carrot fly larvae is a pest that loves to eat the roots – you can take your chances, or you can place a fine mesh over the carrots to protect them. Carrots may need watering in particularly dry spells, but be careful not to overwater. Once they are ready you can

remove them as you need them to feed your kitchen, and they will also store well in a cool dark place. There is nothing as exciting as pulling up a carrot that has grown well and kids young and old seem to love crunching on these sweet treats with the greenery still attached!

BED 4 – *Peas and broad beans*

All vegetables taste better from your own plot, but I think peas offer the starkest contrast. It is such a pleasure to eat them fresh from the pod as you inspect your garden. Peas are beautifully easy to grow, too – they just require a wee bit of support.

Broad beans are an early cropper, which is good news for a small garden space, as when they have been harvested, you can grow something else in their place. They are best eaten fresh, but will keep for a few days in their pods once picked.

ALL ABOUT SEED SAVING

Try to get into the habit of saving seeds for planting next year. Seeds saved from plants in your own garden will always be adapting to your conditions, soil and challenges – which makes them, year on year, more suited to growing where you are. The custom of seed saving thus allows you to select varieties that suit your soil.

Watch the plants as they grow in your garden through the season, and you will see which ones are strongest. Then, when they go to seed, you simply collect the seed, clean it of debris, then dry and store it for use next year. It really is that simple.

But if you're unsure, experienced gardeners are usually willing to help you to learn how to do tasks such as seed saving. If they garden close to you, then their local knowledge will most likely apply to your plot too – so, why not make friends with them? That way, you can also share and exchange your saved seeds with them and other friends and neighbours.

Most of all, enjoy the process. Growing plants, feeding your kitchen and being a part of the yearly cycles is an honour and the rewards are a bounty of fresh veggies, plus healthier soil and a more protected environment. Gardening really is good for you – in fact, time spent gardening at your hut could be considered golden!

THE ART OF THE ALLOTMENT HUT

City allotments, those charming parcels of urban land, serve as sanctuaries for industrious souls to nurture the earth, their skilled green fingers coaxing life from the soil. Allotments are a standout example of how important access to the natural world is for city people. Within these patchworked oases, flowers bloom in vibrant hues, fruit trees stretch their branches towards the sky, and nourishing veggies are harvested. It was in the late nineteenth century that the concept of garden allotments blossomed, as disused urban land was granted to the poor in small lots, giving them the means to cultivate their own sustenance. In the wake of rapid industrialisation and the absence of a comprehensive welfare state, these acts of Victorian philanthropy extended meaningful, developmental aid to those in need, strengthening self-sufficiency skills and conferring significant nutritional and health benefits.

In the aftermath of the First World War, a shift in priority directed the allocation of allotments to those valiant people who had served their country, some of whom had gained agricultural expertise through their wartime endeavours. There was also a resounding call to expand the accessibility of allotments to the wider public, and the uptake was strong.

As these invaluable plots have matured in our city communities, an evolution of allotment huts has quietly taken place within them. These humble sheds, though distinct in nature and usage, are reminiscent of their historical counterparts – the residential huts. They, too, are born of resourcefulness and ingenuity. Constructed from salvaged and scavenged materials, these huts – whether immaculate or intriguingly ramshackle – stand as captivating structures, each with its own unique story to tell. The spirit of the hutting movement resonates in the parallel of these structures, as an allotment adorned with a cute hut becomes an inviting haven. Here, the convergence of greenhouse and shed creates a gathering place where camaraderie flourishes alongside carnations and tomatoes, conversations rise and fall over mugs of tea, and shelter from the rain becomes a cherished commodity, nay luxury!

Over the course of the twentieth century, the popularity of allotments in Scotland fluctuated. Yet, in recent years, the allure of these bite-sized plots of land and their wee huts has surged once more. Such is their appeal that certain regions have waiting lists spanning years, proof of how our hearts yearn for that hands-on connection with nature that comes from the simple act of tending to the earth. Perhaps an allotment with a hut will be your entry into the world of hutting – it seems like a logical next step to me!

So, what to do with the fruits of your labour? Here are some ideas of how to transform your hut produce...

BAKED STRAWBERRY JAM

In the autumn we love to get Granny's old jelly pan out in the hut and boil up a load of brambles, a few rosehips and rowans with sugar on the stove to make her Bramble Jelly. The ritual of gathering and boiling fruits, then decanting the jelly jam into jars to store for the year ahead is so comforting and satisfying – with the bonus that it fills your whole home with an irresistibly sweet and fruity aroma.

However, you will pick strawberries from the garden much earlier in the summer and in abundance – making this no-fuss baked jam recipe a real winner. It is delicious on toast, in cakes or even in a trifle. The baking process really concentrates the sweet strawberry flavour yet uses considerably less sugar than conventional jam recipes – and, if you freeze it, think how happy you'll be to delve into your store of this summer treat as the season shifts towards cooler days.

INGREDIENTS

500g strawberries
100g sugar
1 tbsp balsamic vinegar
1 tsp vanilla extract
Pinch of salt

METHOD

Preheat the oven to 180°C (fan).

Remove the stalks and chop the strawberries into quarters, then place in an ovenproof dish. Add the sugar, balsamic vinegar, vanilla and salt and give it a good mix, spreading the strawberries evenly.

Now bake for about 90 minutes, stirring occasionally. Keep an eye on the jam towards the end of the 90 minutes, as the baking time will depend on the water content of the fruit. You want the liquid to evaporate, leaving a lovely jammy consistency.

Sterilise your jars by baking them in the oven for a few minutes, then pot up the baked jam while it is still warm. Leave it to cool in the jars before eating. You can keep it in the fridge for a few weeks; alternatively, you can put it in Tupperware and freeze it.

THE ART OF HUTTING

HUTTER'S HACK

THE ZEER POT

Have you heard of the Zeer pot? It is a brilliant creation designed to maintain the coolness of its contents. Think of it as a DIY flowerpot fridge! It is an ideal solution for extending the shelf life of perishable items in situations where a fridge is unavailable – such as when you're at your hut on a scorching hot day – but please be aware that it may not be suitable for storing meat.

The roots of the Zeer pot can be traced back thousands of years to the ingenious Ancient Egyptians. It operates on the principle of evaporative cooling and continues to be widely used in many hot countries.

It is such a straightforward process, so why not create your own Zeer pot? You will need:
- 2 terracotta pots (one larger and one smaller)
- Sand
- A pallet

METHOD

Begin by dismantling the pallet and laying the stripped boards on the ground. Use the larger pot as a template to trace a circle, which will serve as the lid for your Zeer pot. Cut the boards accordingly and assemble them with a handle, using nails.

Next, line the larger pot with sand and position the smaller pot inside, ensuring they are level at the top. Centre the inner pot and fill the space between the pots with sand.

Now, whenever you are at the hut and want to keep items cool, simply place them in your Zeer pot after you have poured cold water into the sand.

HUTTER'S CHUTNEY

Since most hutters visit their hut intermittently, gardening can present some problems. Vegetable patches appreciate regular attention, which means they can become more difficult to manage if you are not there very often. Or perhaps there are deer, rabbits or other hungry critters ready and waiting to sample your fayre before you are ready to harvest.

This is why, at our hut, we have opted to plant fruit trees, as they are low maintenance, a protective fence around them will keep the deer off and, best of all, if we are lucky they will yield armfuls of fruit!

As we like to say, if life gives you plums, make chutney. It is a delicious, tangy, spicy and sweet condiment that can be relied on to elevate both a sophisticated cheese board and the most everyday of sandwiches, or give a fabulous oomph to a baked potato. This recipe makes five or six jars, which you can then keep in the cupboard for a few weeks.

INGREDIENTS

800g plums
300g onions
2 celery stalks
100g raisins
100g cranberries
200g muscovado sugar
1 tsp crushed dried chilli
4 dark cardamom pods
1 tsp salt
2 tsp yellow mustard seeds
150ml cider vinegar
150ml malt vinegar
2 cinnamon sticks
1 star anise

METHOD

Remove the stones from the plums, and cut them into halves. Peel and chop your onions. Add all the ingredients to a pan and bring to the boil. Then turn the heat down and simmer for an hour – stirring occasionally so it doesn't stick to the pan. Sterilise your jars by baking them in the oven for a few minutes, then when both the jars and the chutney are cool, spoon the mixture in and seal.

CHAPTER FIVE

FIRE

An teine a nì duine dha fhèin, 's e choir a gharadh ris.

It is your right to warm yourself at your own fire.

What is it about a fire that draws us? The alchemy of the process of combustion is quite simply mesmerising – and, of course, incredibly useful. Early humans would surely have first encountered this magical, frightening force when ground fires were started by accidents of nature. I like to think of them cautiously following the fire, respecting its power, aware of the danger, yet watching carefully from afar as flames tore through the land. Fascinated, as they witnessed its destructive power. Then, eventually, as the fire died down to a gentle smoulder their bravery would grow and they would move forward to find things in its wake, learning about its impact in the process. Charred tree trunks, molten metals, smoking shrubs arising from the earth and perhaps the first taste of cooked meat from unlucky carcasses left behind. Imagine the wonder these early humans would have felt in igniting a branch to create a rudimentary torch, giving them the power to transport this mysterious force. No wonder they figured out how to harness its power and create the first sparks to use its magnificent energy. Humanity evolves, but our relationship with fire is ancient and unchanging; the simple truths about our human connection to it remain constant.

When we were little, I shared a room with my brothers Mark and Robin for a few years – and in it there was a fireplace. On those rare, special occasions when it cackled to life, such as during the Christmas holidays or if any of us were ill, I can vividly recall the enchanting dance of the flickering firelight on the ceiling and the radiance of its warmth filling the snug room.

There is nothing quite like drifting off to sleep while gazing at the fading embers, their gentle glow offering the last of their comfort and illumination. The fire is now my favourite thing about staying in the hut. One room, the fireplace at its heart – this essential element enables the enchantment of hutting. In fact, I would say that the stove is an indispensable necessity for any hut. It provides the means to cook food, is a source of warmth and offers a focal point for the cèilidh.

At the MacQueen hut, my dad made the decision to install a wood-burning cookstove. It is arguably a bit too big for the space, but there is method in his madness, which comes down to how my parents use the hut. Most of the time they are day trippers, so the Esse Ironheart he chose is perfect for them as it heats the space quickly and they can cook lunch on it before heading home. It's a reliable workhorse of a stove that adds a touch of charm to the hut.

HUTTER'S HACK

DEVICES FOR YOUR STOVETOP

My hutter's list of stovetop devices to maximise your stove!

KETTLE

This old faithful keeps us plied with tea and hot water for the dishes. You can't beat the cheery noise of the whistle telling you the water is boiling. My top tip is to have flasks handy to store boiling water for later.

TOASTING RACK

We have a brilliantly simple toasting rack from the Aga cookshop; it is so effective for use with a hotplate and makes perfect toast.

CAST IRON POTATO COOKER

This wee device is for use on top of any stove. It uses the surface heat, meaning a hot plate isn't essential. It's not fast, but it is a green and energy-efficient way of cooking the best crispy baked potatoes ever. Slow cooked for a few hours, they are perfection!

TOASTIE MAKER

There are various toastie makers on the market but the one we have from Jean Patrique is braw for use on the stove top. It makes for a tasty addition to the hut lunch menu options.

COFFEE POT

I honestly don't think I would enjoy hutting if I couldn't have a decent cup of coffee and so the Bialetti coffee pot is my best pal. I use mine on the hotplate or a gas ring.

JELLY PAN

Why not go retro and get a jelly pan just like your granny used to use. Great for making jam, jelly and chutney on your stove top or outside on an open fire.

THE STOVE

Any hutters lucky enough to stay in a hut with a mezzanine area will contest that sleeping up in the rafters when the stove is lit can be uncomfortably warm at times. There is always that moment of dilemma in the early evening when you want to put another log on the fire because it is so pleasant and cosy, but you also know you shouldn't if you want the temperature up the ladder to be at acceptable level for bedtime. To log or not to log, that is the real question…

While all wood-burning stoves produced and sold since 2022 must – under DEFRA's Clean Air Strategy 2019 – comply with ecodesign regulations that ensure minimum energy-efficiency standards, owning an older stove is not illegal. And on my *The Art of Hutting* tour of huts, I certainly saw all kinds of stoves in different shapes, sizes, ages, makes and models.

So, as the stove is always going to be the heart of your hut, it is worth investing in one that will suit your needs – and that you truly love in terms of its functionality, aesthetics and charm. Trust me, you are going to spend a lot of time looking at it.

Whichever stove you choose, I can guarantee that tending to your fire will become a joyful obsession. You will become familiar with the old saying that wood warms you thrice… once when you chop it, once when you stack it, and once when you burn it.

THE ART OF THE WOODPILE

A freshly cut log weighing one kilogram can contain up to a pint of water. This means that, if you try to burn it when wet, it will take a lot of energy from the fire and create a lot more smoke. All of which is bad for your stove, gives off a poor yield and means your woodpile is not working for you as it should.

The benefits of managing a woodpile so that your logs have time to properly dry and season are astounding. The yield from dry wood is considerably higher and burning clean, quality logs helps reduce air pollution. There is nothing quite like the satisfaction of entering the winter period knowing that your wood store is full of split, stacked, dry, ready-to-burn logs. If you are able to work two seasons ahead, you will ensure they are always perfect.

There is an art to seasoning wood. For soft woods such as pine, a year of seasoning is good, and for hard woods such as oak a two-year period is desirable. It is therefore important – and immensely satisfying – to work ahead. Experience will teach you what will work best for you, in your area, and with the variety of wood you have available.

As a general guide, it is advisable to aim to lift fallen wood – boughs of trees that are already down – or take standing trees that have already died. But please be sure to leave some fallen boughs as habitat for woodland creatures. If you are cutting down living

trees from a sustainable source, then aim to fell during the dormant winter months; that is, before the sap rises in the early spring, as this will reduce the wood's moisture content.

Cutting shorter lengths of logs will help in the drying process and wee logs are often ideal for the small stoves commonly found in huts. You can split the logs with an axe and stack them raised off the ground; old pallets are ideal for this purpose. Stack your pile loosely: this ensures that air can circulate between the logs, which is crucial to allow them to dry well.

We have a simple shed with a tin roof as our log store. It doesn't have any sides, which allows for free movement of air while keeping the rain off. I have seen logs simply stacked against the side of huts to dry; a south-facing prospect is superb for sunshine to help them dry out. If you don't have room for a woodpile, then you can create a vertical stack within your hut space, and allow the heat from your stove to speed up the drying process. Stacking logs is a fun job that everyone in the family can help with, but of course take real care if using saws or an axe.

ESSENTIAL AXE SAFETY TIPS!
1. Maintain a safety circle when working with an axe.
2. Use a chopping block for splitting wood.
3. Ensure your axe is well maintained for the job.
4. Store your axe safely when it is not in use.

As a hutter with a stove, you'll always be on the lookout for firewood. At our hut, my dad runs a hybrid approach to the wood situation. We bring in offcuts of wood which he gets from a local joiner – and this goes a long way to feeding the stove, especially with kindling. If you find a source of free wood like this, then be sure to avoid treated woods, as burning painted or varnished wood will most likely create dirty smoke which is bad for the stove, the environment and your health. My dad also works with the woods themselves, as it were, to harvest responsibly, focusing on fallen wood, or trees that will replenish in a short time.

HUTTER'S HACK

THE FIERY ART OF LIGHTING YOUR STOVE

Setting a fire is a skill that comes with practice, but you can learn a few tips to help you to get it going for those first few times.

- Use a firelighter, with tinder such as newspaper, dried grass or bark.
- Neatly stack very dry sticks as kindling. Then strike your match.
- The key is to create conditions for a strong core fire, so quickly add smaller-sized sticks around that.
- Keep the stove's flue open to let the fire draw the oxygen it needs to get going. If you don't have a flue, keep the stove door slightly ajar at this stage.
- Add larger logs once the fire is well underway, and close the flue, or the door – to maximise the yield from the logs you are burning.
- Keep the ashes cleared after each fire, and dispose of any hot ashes responsibly. They will start a fire of their own if you don't.

HOW TO MAKE YOUR FIREWOOD CHOICES

Please exercise extreme caution when using saws, axes or working at harvesting wood. It can be dangerous – and any injuries are usually serious. Please ensure, too, that you have permission to harvest wood from the landowner.

When it comes to choosing the best firewood for stoves, several options stand out.

ASH / FRAXINUS EXCELSIOR / UINNSEANN

A top choice for burning in stoves, ash casts a steady flame that emanates abundant heat. Unfortunately, ash trees in Scotland have been afflicted by ash dieback, a windborne fungal disease. As we face the prospect of losing up to 75% of mature ash trees over the next two decades, there may be a lot of ash to cut down for fuel consumption. However, efforts are underway to manage this decline and nurture resilient specimens, fostering hope for future regeneration.

BEECH / FAGUS SYLVATICA / FAIDHBHILE

Beech provides warmth and comfort with its dependable combustion properties, thereby embracing the role of a reliable stove-fueller.

HAWTHORN / CRATAEGUS MONOGYNA / SGÌTHEACH

For those seeking exceptional heat output, hawthorn deserves your attention. Its unhurried burn yields a remarkable amount of warmth, ensuring maximum cosiness. Bush-like and slow-growing, hawthorn thrives when pruned, making it a contender for harvesting in small amounts from mature trees.

PINE / PINUS SYLVESTRI / GIUTHAS

Pine wood unleashes a splendid flame, although one must be mindful of its resin sap, which can cause crackling and popping. The resin content, however, makes it an ideal choice for kindling.

OAK / QUERCUS ROBUR / DARACH

Known for its leisurely burn and modest flames, oak stands as an excellent hardwood firewood selection. Be sure to season oak for at least two years to optimise its performance and ensure a superior combustion experience.

BIRCH / BETULA PENDULA / BEITH

Renowned for its robust flame and generous heat production, birch wood tends to burn swiftly. Consider coupling it with other logs such as oak to prolong the fire's duration. Birch bark is an exceptional tinder that will ignite your fire with ease. Fortunately, birch trees grow relatively fast, allowing for a constant supply when harvested responsibly.

HAZEL / CORYLUS AVELLANA / CALLTAINN

This is a superb choice for firewood, burning swiftly and without spitting. Hazel wood responds favourably to coppicing, enabling winter harvesting for firewood.

ROWAN / SORBUS AUCUPARIA / CAORANN

With its strong folklore tradition in Scotland, rowan is regarded as a good firewood, one which burns well to provide comforting warmth. Its mystical reputation includes the power to ward off evil spirits – leading to a superstition in some parts that it's bad luck to cut down a rowan.

HOW TO FUEL RESPONSIBLY

To truly embrace the diverse possibilities of burning these firewood types in Scotland, consider foraging fallen branches and twigs as kindling. Regardless of your chosen fuel, remember to exercise responsible practices when fuelling your stove.

HUTTER'S HACK

ALL ABOUT FORAGING...
FOR KINDLING

When you go for walks near your hut, keep an eye out for any sticks lying on the ground – they will be naturally seasoned and ready to burn. This is an easy, economical way to ensure you always have kindling to spark the stove. Embrace these gifts as Mother Nature generously furnishes your stove with freebies! Birch bark also works well as tinder, as do fallen pinecones, which are fun to collect.

Trees are a rejuvenating resource, and thoughtful management ensures a continuous supply of firewood for years to come. For example, if felling living trees, then aim to identify those that may be struggling for light, or are suffering from disease. Removing trees of this nature will create space for others to thrive.

A GUIDE TO OUTDOOR FIRES

An outside fire – at a lochside, on the hillside or on the shore – is one of life's greatest pleasures; the perfect way to share time with family and friends.

However, given the risks posed by fires to wildlife and the environment, it is absolutely vital that you follow the countryside code and remain attentive to ensure any outdoor fire you light, at all its stages, is properly under control. Ensuring recreational fires are small, and ideally made in a safe firepit or circle, will help to enable you to keep it under control at all times. In dry periods, you must be critically aware of the danger of fire spreading into grass or nearby brush.

Never, ever leave dying embers – make sure a fire is fully extinguished before leaving it. Douse the fire with water, stir the ashes and continue dousing until you are certain it is completely out. Never light a fire at the base of a living tree as it will damage the tree – and there's a real risk that the leaves above the fire could catch.

Whenever we can, we build a small fire on the beach at the hut and gather to enjoy the special atmosphere it evokes. My dad gets his accordion out and the cèilidh begins. Uncle Stuart likes to make sure everyone has a drink in hand and Coinneach and I are in charge of encouraging a lively singsong. The tideline on the beach is an ideal spot for these fires, as we can make a circle with stones for the fire, there are no obstacles overhead and we can use sea water to douse the embers when we are done.

For children, the tales spun around the fire possess an extraordinary enchantment, weaving a tapestry of memories that seem charged with an ancient alchemy that delights the human spirit. The flickering firelight transforms stories into more than mere words; through the flames, they etch themselves into our hearts. Our oral storytelling traditions have been carried down through the generations in precisely this way – and it is a genuine privilege to belong to this fireside tribe as it continues these customs.

HUTTER'S HACK
THE PERFECT OUTDOOR FIRE

- Create the perimeter of your fire – perhaps with a circle of stones or logs.
- Use a firepit if you have one.
- Be mindful of your surroundings and assess possible hazards – such as dry grass, overhanging trees, nearby structures or any flammable materials.
- Gather firewood – ideally as dry as possible; you won't need lots, keep it small. This is a task where kids love to get involved!
- Firstly, get the core fire going and then carefully add to the stack. Try to make sure sticks cannot fall out of the fire. Never add any accelerants to your fire.
- Maintain your group at a safe distance from the fire when it is at its peak, taking special care of children and any pets.
- Educate young people about the joys and the dangers of fire in the process.
- Keep your wood supply a safe distance from the fire, so that you can gradually add to it and keep it going for longer.
- Use a knife to sharpen some long sticks ready for marshmallow toasting.
- Lastly, never leave embers burning. Ensure the fire is completely out before leaving the site.

TOP TIP! Remember… if you have assessed the dangers and decide the conditions are not safe to light your fire, do not go against your instincts. Save the fire for another day. It is always better to be safe than sorry.

WHERE TO ENJOY A COSY CABIN FIRE

If you fancy a stay in a cabin with a fire, then I recommend these wee beauties. When we stayed, we enjoyed the magic of fire – both inside and out.

Nestled along the tranquil shores of Loch Fyne, the Kabn Company awaits, offering a restful haven where nature takes centre stage. These charming off-grid cabins effortlessly blend minimalist design with their breathtaking surroundings, boasting floor-to-ceiling glass that invites the outside in. Prepare for a truly luxurious hutting experience!

When I visited, what truly set this destination apart was the opportunity to indulge in the gastronomic wonders of the Wilder Kitchen, masterfully curated by chef William Hamer. With a recent stint at the renowned Hiša Franko, a two-Michelin-starred restaurant in Slovenia, Will brings a deep passion for integrating food with fire: watching him cook over the flames is mesmerising. His culinary ethos revolves around championing local suppliers, handpicking the finest organic and sustainable ingredients that harmonise perfectly with the stunning natural environment.

HUTTER'S HACK

HOW TO MAKE YOUR OWN LOG LANTERNS

Get ready to bask in delightful firelight with these enchanting log lanterns. They are not only a breeze to craft but also remarkably effective. As twilight descends and you gather outside your hut, a log lantern will cast a hypnotic glow, providing a cheerfully intimate ambiance for your outdoor cèilidhs. They are so charming in their simplicity: log rounds, deftly cut with a chainsaw, to make a crisscross pattern extending nearly the entire length of the log, stopping approximately 3 inches from the base.

Store the logs by your warm stove for a few weeks so they become bone dry before use. When the time comes to illuminate your outdoor space, choose a safe spot to position the lantern, and place a tiny piece of firelighter in the heart of the crisscross and ignite it. Watch as the chimney effect of the lines cut down the length of the logs draws the fire to the centre, giving a radiant glow.

FAYE'S FIRED AUBERGINE PASTA

Whenever my good pal Faye comes to stay at the hut, we always have this pasta for dinner on the first night. It is next level comfort food, quick and easy to make and quite simply delicious – just what you want after a long journey. I recommend orzo pasta because it doesn't require as much stirring as risotto rice (which also works for this recipe) in the cooking process. This will make enough for two to three people.

INGREDIENTS

2 aubergines
80g smoked pancetta
1 onion
1 leek
2 celery stalks
1 fresh red chilli
250g orzo pasta
500ml chicken stock
50g grated Parmesan
Olive oil, for frying

METHOD

Pierce the aubergines a few times with the tip of a knife and place them in the fire box of your stove, directly onto burning logs – or if you have a gas ring you can scorch them on there. Don't be shy: aubergine has a thick skin and can take a lot of heat. This will give the pulp a lovely smoky flavour and don't be afraid to completely char them, as you will discard the skin later. This will take 12 to 15 minutes in the fire, during which time you can turn them occasionally, thereby testing your poker skills and giving you the chance to check how they are cooking.

While the aubergines are in the fire, you can get everything else ready. Start by frying the pancetta on a medium heat, until crispy and the fat has rendered in the pan. Chop the onion, leek, celery and chilli and add to the pan with a splash of olive oil to soften for 10 minutes or until golden brown.

Add the orzo pasta and stock and leave to simmer for 5 minutes. Your well-fired aubergines should be ready: carefully lift them out and place on a chopping board. Use a sharp knife to remove all the skin and then mix the beautifully cooked pulp into your pan.

Cook for another 5 minutes, then add the Parmesan and leave the pan to sit off the heat with a lid on for a few minutes to let the flavours settle before serving.

PIZZA DOUGH

Sometimes the simplest of meals can be the most enjoyable… and when we have groups of pals visiting at the hut, the Ooni pizza oven is a popular choice. You can cater for most tastes with a range of toppings, and making your own pizza dough is fun and easy.

INGREDIENTS

425g '00' flour or strong white flour
75g semolina flour
1 heaped tsp caster sugar
1x 7g sachet of dried yeast
1 tbsp olive oil
325ml warm water
Large pinch of salt

METHOD

This recipe yields enough dough for four pizzas. Add the flours, sugar and salt to a bowl and mix – then add the yeast and give it another mix. Add the olive oil and the water and bring the dough together. Knead for 10 to 15 minutes to give your arms a proper workout.

You'll know the dough is ready when it bounces back when you push your finger into it. At this point, leave the dough covered with a clean damp tea towel to prove for an hour while it rises and your tummy rumbles in anticipation of the pizza to come!

If fire can make hutting extra special in such a profound manner, it is difficult to consider what else could enhance hut experiences even further? Perhaps another of the elements – water…

CHAPTER SIX

WATER

Chan eil carraig air nach caochail sruth.

There is no rock that a stream can't get past.

Huts and water are a seductive combination, with beach huts, river huts and fishing huts all commonplace throughout Scotland. I think we all appreciate water's calming influence, its potential for sports and for fishing of all kinds and, of course, who can resist watching as the waves roll in off a stormy sea, the rush of a river in full spate or dark clouds passing over a broody loch? Now, with the evolution and return of residential huts, many would-be hutters are looking to coastline, lochside and riverbank as potential sites.

BEACH HUTTIES AT HOPEMAN

On the picturesque Moray coast, there exists a community of traditional seaside "hutties" that has flourished over the generations. Nestled along the crest of the dunes, are the vibrant Hopeman beach huts. As you stroll along the path, you will discover forty-four well-maintained but uniquely sized and shaped wee huts, each adorned in a kaleidoscope of colours. Each hut is so eclectic and individual that you never know quite what charming colour palette or delightful quirk awaits in the next one.

Intrigued by the sight of an open door at hut number 26, I couldn't resist making a beeline towards it. To my surprise, I stumbled upon a lively parliament of three older gents. James, Sandy and Paul warmly welcomed me into their midst; without hesitation they invited me to take a seat and join their conversation.

Stepping inside, I was enveloped by a homely atmosphere. The interior boasted a gas hob, ample chairs for everyone, a side table, walls adorned with artwork, and a breathtaking view through the double doors to the blue expanse of sea beyond.

Every day except for Sundays, the men convene at James's huttie at 10.45 a.m. This is their beloved meeting spot, where there are no boundaries when it comes to their discussions. Except, of course, "coveting your neighbour's wife," they chuckle with infectious laughter.

"Actually," Sandy interjects, "we tell our wives that we discuss the political situation in North Korea!" This quip prompts a chorus of amusement from the group, while James prepares a round of tea on the gas hob.

WORLDS OF WATER

The mere presence of water – whether it be the sea, a river, a loch or a stream – truly seems to have a calming effect on the soul. Spending time near these tranquil natural settings brings us a sense of well-being and, fortunately for us Scots, we are blessed with an astonishing abundance of picturesque watery locales.

Did you know, for example, that Scotland boasts over 30,000 lochs? These vary from vast expanses of deep water such as Loch Ness and Loch Lomond to much smaller lochans nestled in the hills. The Scottish coastline stretches an estimated 18,743 kilometres, and it is home to more than nine hundred islands. Additionally, there are over 125,000 kilometres of rivers and streams, encompassing highland burns and broad lowland rivers such as the magnificent Tay. Inspiring terrain indeed, whose beguiling allure some lucky hutters have been unable to resist as they built their huts.

The historical relationship between society and the seaside is intriguing. In the late 1700s, cold water was believed to possess healing properties, and the idea of it as a panacea for various ailments had garnered attention, prompting people to flock to the coast in great numbers. The sea offered a sense of adventure and was free to all. Consequently, sea bathing gained huge popularity across all social classes.

The development of an extensive railway system across the UK throughout the 1800s made travel to far-off destinations possible. As the network grew, so too did the popularity of seaside towns and villages. These once difficult-to-reach places morphed into popular tourist destinations – even my hometown of Oban experienced this surge in popularity when the West Highland Line finally reached the Gateway to the Isles in

1880. In front of Oban's grand Alexandra Hotel, you can still see remnants of the walls of the old bathing pool built for seawater dooks.

In the nineteenth century, horse-drawn carts known as "bathing machines" revolutionised beach recreation. These mobile changing rooms provided privacy to bathers, and Queen Victoria herself possessed a rather fancy one. In July 1847, her bathing machine at Osborne Beach on the Isle of Wight preserved her royal modesty as she ventured into the sea.

During the 1890s, demand grew for mixed bathing, driven in part by the practices already prevalent in northern European and American seaside resorts. As societal norms shifted, allowing individuals to comfortably stroll along the beach in their bathing costumes, the need for bathing machines gradually diminished. Consequently, purpose-built day huts started to emerge, replacing the wheeled contraptions of the past.

Nowadays, the unpretentious huts at the fishing village of Hopeman serve as gathering places where passersby become acquaintances and news is exchanged with enthusiasm. On sunny days, most of these huts open their doors, welcoming local people to the seaside. The village dogs are particularly fond of paying visits, too, hoping to snag a biscuit or two.

"There's aye somebody pops in, ken?" James remarks with a twinkle in his eyes, and as if on cue there is a tap at the door and a waggy wee dog comes in for a drink of water from the bowl in the corner.

James was born and bred in Hopeman, and spent his entire working life at sea, fishing for white fish in Peterhead, Aberdeen and even along Scotland's west coast. Reflecting on the changing times, he remarks, "There's nothing like the number of boats that used to work out of here. There were twenty-four boats or so, and now there are only two." As he prepares toasted butteries for his companions, James spots the Fishery Protection boat on the horizon. This prompts him to grab the binoculars hanging from a nearby hook. "They're heading west now," he comments, sharing this latest sighting with a sense of familiarity. I get the impression not many boats can pass here without these three spotting their movements.

Having patiently waited for a beach hut for over a decade, James has now enjoyed his own little haven for fifteen years. Each year, he and his fellow hutties contribute around £50 each for the community land on which their huts stand. A set of agreed rules ensures the upkeep of these retreats that have been here for over seventy-five years now, and guarantees them a secure future.

The succession of beach huts runs through families, often favouring Hopeman residents when vacancies arise on the waiting list. If anyone wants to sell their hut, there is a fair system in place whereby a local joiner appraises the value of the hut itself rather than the site, keeping the prices affordable.

But the benefits of a beach hut are priceless. They grant unrestricted access to the beach regardless of the weather. They serve as storage spaces for seaside paraphernalia such as wetsuits, towels, buckets, spades, games and woolly hats to fend off the chill. They always have plenty of fold-up chairs, perfect for hosting lively cèilidhs and BBQs on blissful summer nights.

As I bid farewell to the men at hut number 26, James hands me a John o' Groats shell, a type of cowrie shell he found on the beach. "That's a *groatie buckie*, for luck!" he exclaims, offering it to me with a smile. My heart is warmed once more by the generous camaraderie of these three friends in their wee huttie, and by the coastal charm of Hopeman.

FINDHORN BEACH HUTS – MORAY

In 2017, new beach huts were built elsewhere on the Moray coastline, just a few miles down the road at Findhorn. Standing proudly near the site where historical beach huts once graced the shore, these additions bring a sense of joyous nostalgia. Uniform in structure, they only differ in their sprightly hues, creating a rainbow cluster against the stony beachfront. While the price tag attached to these huts stirred some local controversy, the architect staunchly defended their hefty £25,000 cost, assuring sceptics that they were "as strong as houses and would grow in value".

And he might not be wrong. Beach huts across the UK have witnessed a staggering surge in prices in the twenty-first century, meaning that the cost of these Findhorn huts is still well below the national average.

For Manda, the desire for her own beach hut has been a lifelong dream. As a teenager, her family embarked on a new chapter, leaving Essex behind and immersing themselves in the hectic life of running a Blackpool hotel. Amid the dazzling new world of ballroom dancers, candyfloss, bingo, beaches, the illuminations and the Tower, Manda found solace in visits to her aunt's beach hut. It was there that she first tasted the essence of a truly contented family, as the enchanting ritual of brewing tea within the wooden haven cast a spell upon her heart.

Years later, now a grandmother herself, Manda has turned her dream into a reality. Her very own beach hut has become a daily sanctuary. Within its welcoming embrace, she adores moments with friends, brewing tea and kindling small fires; a remnant of her time as a Girl Guide. Music resonates, interwoven with laughter as precious memories are forged. Each visit holds its own stillness, a unique tapestry of experiences waiting to unfurl.

There is something timeless and primal about gathering around a crackling fire on a beach, as the sky gradually surrenders to twilight's caress. For Manda, the true blessing lies in the time spent with her family at the beach hut. Witnessing her sons fly kites, passing the art on to her beloved grandson, and providing a simple shelter where babies can be fed and watered, the beach hut becomes a place of togetherness. Laughter prompted by the friendly competitiveness of boules, Scrabble and card games fills the air.

Manda describes her beach hut as a steadfast friend, ready to embrace her at any time of the day or night, without question. As she swings open the double doors, settles into her comforting rattan chair, and allows the rhythm of the waves to imprint their melody upon her, she reflects on whether the hut has lived up to her expectations. Without hesitation, she affirms that it has more than surpassed them, transforming not only her life but also the lives of those around her.

WATER THERAPY

The benefits of hot and then cold water plunging can be considerable, although not recommended for everyone and especially not for those who might have heart disease, high blood pressure, diabetes or are pregnant. Children should also be supervised at all times.

Many believe that taking a cold water plunge is a source of natural pain management, an immune system booster and may help with fostering a healthier mental state. I like to combine cold and warmth: I definitely find it easier to go in the cold water if I know that there is a nice warm tub to climb into afterwards! That goes for sea swims too…

A hot tub at a hut requires an onsite water source so that you can change the water regularly. If you can arrange that, then a wood-fired tub really is the best hutting luxury ever. But always take care not to enter water that is too hot.

Water-gathering systems for huts are a genius way to collect rainwater; such a system is well worth incorporating into the design of your hut. Many use elaborate systems of interconnected guttering, barrels and water butts to make the most of our abundant rainfall. You will also find this especially useful if you plan to grow veggies and need a ready source of water for your plants.

THE FISHERMEN'S HUTS OF ISLAY

A short stride over the hill from the bustling village of Port Ellen in Islay lies a picturesque bay adorned with quaint fishermen's huts that serve their purpose to this day. This bonnie haven, once known as Port nam Bàtaichean – Port of the boats – holds a significant place in the island's history, owing to the arrival in the early 1800s of Irish immigrants seeking employment in the thriving fishing industry. Within this wee bay, countless families toiled diligently upon the rocky shores, landing, gutting and drying the day's catch, preparing it for the awaiting markets.

In bygone times, Islay boasted a much larger population, with an estimated 15,000 inhabitants in the nineteenth century, compared to the modest count of around 3,500 in 2023. As the bay grew in prominence, it garnered a new local name, Poll na h-Eala, or the Swan's Pool, in tribute to a bereaved solo swan that once made its home there.

This little bay, with its handful of stone-built, jetty-like piers, resonates with the whispers of hardworking fishermen past and present and is still frequented by locals who keep boats there, store their gear in the huts and work out of this picturesque harbour. One such is fisherman Chris Jamieson, who walks over the hill from the family home he shares with his wife Lynne to the hut every day. It means he can store items from his boat here and this makes fishing trips easier. Oilskins and creels are ever ready if the shipping forecast indicates favourable fishing weather!

RIVER HUTS – THE ISLE OF LEWIS

The river huts at Grimersta Lodge, Isle of Lewis and Uig Lodge at Ciste an Fhorsa are iconic stone huts where those on fishing trips can shelter from the elements and enjoy the river. They are situated amid spectacular Hebridean scenery and not too far from where the famous Lewis Chessmen were discovered in the sands of Ardroil in 1831.

If you like to fish, perhaps these little riverside huts will offer you shelter as you have your lunch and prepare your rod and flies. You can buy permits to fish these rivers and many other estates in the Hebrides and throughout the Highlands. Salmon, grilse and sea trout enter the river and loch system from late May and the main run is traditionally at its height in mid-July, but fresh run fish occur until the end of the season on 15 October. There is also excellent wild brown trout fishing on innumerable lochs.

Grimersta Lodge
www.grimersta.com
Instagram @grimersta_estate

Uig Lodge
www.uiglodge.co.uk
Instagram @uiglodge

HUTTER'S HACK

BIRCH TAPPING FOR BEGINNERS

There is a sweet spot for harvesting a special arboreal treat – during the period preceding the rising of the sap in birch trees, just as they prepare to burst forth with spring foliage. For approximately four weeks, if timed right, a gentle tap applied at the base of a mature birch tree allows for the collection of a remarkable substance with an understandably woody flavour. This fresh and unusual liquid is a springtime delicacy which will invigorate beverages as a tonic, or – when gathered in sufficient quantities – it can be distilled into a light sugar syrup in a process akin to that employed with maple sap.

When selecting a birch tree to tap, be sure to choose one that has not been tapped in the previous two-year period – this way you will not cause any damage to the tree. Carefully drill a hole at a 45-degree angle, which reaches about 5cm in depth, to ensure a smooth flow of sap downwards and outward. Taps are available online, or alternatively, a length of 4mm-diameter tubing can serve the same purpose. You can simply use a bucket or similar container to capture this precious liquid.

Coinneach and I take real pleasure in savouring this tonic as a dram, or we use it as a delectable glaze to adorn freshly baked buns.

TOP TIP! If making Birch syrup, the sap should be processed at lower temperatures to help to keep the sugars in the liquid from caramelising, which can give the syrup a slightly burnt taste. Begin by bringing the evaporation pan to a gentle boil, then drop the heat to a rolling simmer and reduce to around 20% of the original amount. The syrup will thicken when cooling – store in sterilised jars, and enjoy this unusual treat.

WEE RAB'S HUT TODDY

When you envisage a hot toddy, you think of whisky and Scotland, right? Well, it may surprise you to find out that the name is neither Scottish, nor was the original tipple made with our national drink *uisge-beatha* – "the water of life"! Instead, it seemingly has its roots in India. At the time of the British occupation a drink named *taddy* in Hindi – made from fermented palm sap with spices – became popular with the colonisers, who took the idea back to the UK with them. Over time the original *taddy* has become the beloved warm and spicy dram of today.

The beauty of hot toddies is that they can make you feel better if you have a cold, and make you feel good if you are cold! Given our winter climate, it was surely destined to become a Scottish thing. The hot toddy in all its forms is the perfect drink for the hut – especially in winter when the stove is on and heating water in the kettle is easy. Whenever Robyn visits the hut, she makes her tasty Hut Toddy in the wee metal teapot on the stove and we just keep topping up the water in the spice mix, then sip the night away! You can use any whisky you like, but we always have a bottle of Jura 10 on the go.

INGREDIENTS

Boiling water
1 tbsp honey
Orange rind – 2 thick cuts, and a twist of the juice
Lemon rind – 2 thick cuts, and a twist of the juice
1 cinnamon stick
5 green cardamom pods
10 cloves
3 peppercorns
A double dram of whisky

METHOD

First add boiling water to the teapot or pan, then put all your ingredients in except the whisky – as you don't want the alcohol to evaporate. Let the flavours infuse, just like you would with any tea. After 10 minutes, the toddy mixture will be ready to pour in with your dram. It's restorative if you are feeling under the weather, but a hot toddy is best enjoyed when you are well, sipped and savoured with a good friend. Slàinte mhòr and many more!

CHAPTER SEVEN

Huts About Scotland

Mar gum biodh cearc air tòir nid.

Like a hen in search of a nest.

No one knows exactly how many huts there are in Scotland today, and certainly the idea of Reforesting Scotland's campaign for A Thousand Huts is both notional and aspirational with everyone involved ever hopeful that the numbers will one day sit in line with those of our Northern European neighbours or our Canadian cousins, where access to cabin culture is high.

Scotland has an estimated population of 5.5 million people in 2023. If we consider that one hut can comfortably serve between one and twenty family members and friends – for regular trips, weekends, holidays and gatherings – then we are going to need many more huts!

I am inspired by the many new hutting initiatives which have taken place since 2014. Some are new communities – each with its own unique model and version of how hutting in groups can evolve. Then there are others who are more aptly described as hermit hutters, like my dad. That is not to say that they necessarily always frequent their huts alone, but that their huts do stand in glorious solitude in the landscape.

THE HERMIT HUTTER

I met Ninian in a layby, on a single-track road at the edge of an area of forested land that he owns in Fife. He directed me to reverse into a wee space between tree trunks and I was impressed that, thanks to his guidance, my car door opened neatly between two pine trees and I was able to step out. Ninian smiled, then warmly shook my hand before leading the way into the woods.

As we walked and talked, I took to him immediately; he is charismatic and knowledgeable about the hutting movement, having written down "A thousand huts" and then pitched the idea at a "Soap Box session" at Reforesting Scotland's 2010 Gathering at Loch Torridon – immediately attracting the backing of Karen Grant, Bernard Planterose, Donald McPhillimy and others who saw the potential for a campaign.

He bends to pick a handful of wood sorrel or *Greim Saighdeir* – the soldier's snack as it is known in Gaelic – and we chew on its nutty flavour as we march through the trees.

Ninian's family have lived in this part of the Kingdom of Fife for generations and his favourite place on the planet is where we are headed: his simple wee hut. When we arrived, I was delighted by the hut's charm – and surprised to see smoke coming out of the chimney. "My friend Alex is staying for a while," Ninian told me.

As we approach the hut's small, decked porch, Alex is working with a hammer and chisel, carving a poem onto a granite block. The words are those of "The Bright Field" by R.S. Thomas, the Welsh poet who died in 2000. His work is exquisite: intricate and somehow befitting of the scene. Alex is a calm and gentle man, and I watch carefully as he demonstrates how he etches a letter into the stone.

"Ninian kindly lets me stay at the hut sometimes," he explains softly. "I like being here, because I am very drawn to contemplative prayer, and this is a very quiet place where I can deepen that practice."

I enjoy our meeting and note the peaceful aura surrounding the hut and the two friends. As I read it, the essence of the poem seems to be about being present enough, still enough, grateful enough to really encounter the gift each moment offers. I think how it echoes the ethos of hutting itself. Huts help us to be present, to be still and to feel grateful – and it is one of the loveliest things about hutters that they are often willing to share their space with others and take pleasure in witnessing them enjoy their time at the hut.

As we head back to the cars, I thank Ninian for the tour, and for his own thoughtful contemplations on hutting. I drive away gladdened in my heart; he is an asset to the movement, for sure!

THE LADY FARMER OF THE SOLWAY COAST

Lee Paton exudes the true spirit of the hutting ethos; she radiates warmth, kindness, and a genuine passion for sharing. Her upbringing at Old Torr Farm on the enchanting Solway Coast, alongside her brother Ross, forms a strong connection to the sun-kissed southern shores of Scotland. Our visit was blessed with a cracker of a day, where the sun's golden rays bathed the beach and blue skies stretched over to the tidal island of Hestan.

Their father acquired the farm in 1947, at which point it already boasted a collection of huts situated within its grounds. By the time Lee and Ross were born in the 1960s, most of the huts had already gone, but as kids they used to go and visit one family who had kept their hut going. That was Michael's parents, and now he is the last hutter standing from the original set. He has witnessed the remarkable evolution of no less than three huts on his own plot, a testament to his love of hut life and culture. The outdoor stove at the back of his hut was built by his father, and Michael still uses it to cook on for his kids and grandkids whenever they visit.

Lee's attendance at a Hutters' Rally in Kirkcaldy back in 2016 had a profound effect on her. It was there that she heard speakers talking about the creation of hut sites

and thus was inspired to make that a reality back at the farm. She was propelled into extensive research, fuelled by a desire to rebuild the lost huts of Torr and establish a new community on their farmland, a place that had so warmly welcomed hutters in the past. Drawing from her father's experiences with huts, Lee understood that these humble abodes could seamlessly coexist with the working farm, while fostering a sharing ethos in the way the land is used.

Finally, following much careful consideration by Lee and the planners, permission was granted in September 2018, solidifying the path forward for Lee's vision to blossom and flourish. Now there are seven huts on the farm again, including Lee's very own one, which she uses for wee ultra-local staycation sleepovers with her grandchildren and family. It really does seem that on Old Torr Farm everyone is a winner. I can't help but think how the hutting world needs more people like Lee Paton to be its patrons and advocates!

THE ENCAMPMENT – CLYDE VALLEY

In 2018, I had the pleasure of meeting Louise Witter, an ambitious and driven individual, at her newly acquired thirty-two acre wild forestry site. The land featured the remnants of a Roman camp, adding an intriguing historical touch. Louise had a bold plan in mind – to establish huts at Camp Wood. Her vision was to create one of Scotland's first-ever commercial hutting sites, comprising sixteen huts, one of which would be for community use. I was captivated by her determination and can-do attitude.

Despite experiencing a series of failed site-purchase deals that had cost her money without yielding any results, Louise made the courageous decision to purchase the woods without even seeing them. It was a now-or-never moment for her, and her bid was successful, marking the beginning of her journey to establish The Encampment Huts.

Louise invited me to explore the bare site with her, so together with Seòras, who's always up for an adventure, we ventured into the Clyde Valley. Nestled between the town of Lanark and the motorway, The Encampment offers both ease of access to Scotland's central belt and a sense of seclusion once one is immersed in the forest, with its gorgeous views of Tinto Hill to the east. Still, the site presented numerous challenges, but Louise's pragmatic mindset enabled her to see beyond the idyllic concept of log cabins in the woods. She swiftly turned her attention to practical considerations, such as parking arrangements, access paths, the complex topography of the former forestry

site, preservation of the scheduled monument of the Roman camp ruins, and the need to ensure minimal disruption to the natural habitat of badgers, foxes and other wildlife. As we spoke, the list of challenges seemed endless.

Five years later, Louise and I returned to The Encampment on a warm, sunny day. Seòras was at our heels again – naturally! We met in the car park, where Louise filled a barrel with water from the tap by the gate, and we strolled along the newly constructed paths towards the huts. Nearly all of them had been successfully erected. The transformation astonished me: I couldn't help but be deeply impressed.

Louise, normally a true city dweller, initially found the forest to be an intimidating prospect, both as a lifestyle choice and a terrain to conquer. Pioneering a business model centred around a hutting lifestyle was a bold move. However, the potential to fill a gap in the market soon became evident – given that few individuals transition from not having a hut to immediately building one from scratch. Louise has played a key role in providing a suitable site for aspiring hutters – with access to a site undoubtedly the most significant barrier to new huts in Scotland today.

The Encampment revolves around hutting. Its essence is that of a lifestyle which embraces simple wooden structures and fosters a connection with nature. However, this remarkable place is also about cultivating a sense of community and, from a business perspective, ensuring a return on investment. When I asked about her success in generating profit, Louise smiled and shrugged her shoulders. Hutting sites, it seems, are not a quick path to financial gain, but rather a slow-burning endeavour. Nevertheless, the hutters do pay ground rents and the value of her forest has undeniably appreciated. If it were ever put on the market, it would be considered a rare and exceptional property. Perhaps, in the end, the true measure of success for Louise's forest is indeed a utopian one – to nurture an environment that expands the happiness quotient of hutters.

Louise's original vision was for the forest to become a retreat – a space for reflection and rejuvenation. Now, with most of the huts occupied by tenant hutters enjoying the security of long leases, I could witness the community settling in and evolving in its own distinctive way. Each hutting site possesses a distinct personality, and The Encampment exuded a peaceful, laid-back energy. I eagerly anticipate future visits to witness its growth and development in years to come.

184 | THE ART OF HUTTING

HUTTERS AT THE ENCAMPMENT

BILLY AND SUSI

When constructing their hut, this couple worked with a local cooperative that aimed to nurture the skill sets of women passionate about building. A notable mark of inclusivity and the ability of hutting projects to empower individuals, their hut was built almost entirely by an all-female team – with Billy as an ally.

RACHEL AND CRAIG

What makes the experience even more delightful for these hutting grandparents is the fact that their daughter also owns a hut within The Encampment, allowing them to share the joy of visits with their grandchildren. Their hutting life is testament to the deep-rooted familial bonds that flourish in huts.

CARNOCK WOOD – FIFE

An exciting new development is underway in the hutting world, and it is taking place at Carnock Wood near Saline in Fife. More than six hundred people applied for one of the twelve plots – showcasing an extraordinary demand for a hut of one's own. Leases and a code of conduct have been drawn up with the help of Reforesting Scotland, between hutters and Forestry and Land Scotland.

As the primary provider of outdoor recreation in Scotland, this Scottish government agency holds the responsibility of managing our forestry land. With an annual influx of over ten million visitors, they generate substantial tourism revenue for the broader Scottish economy. Their mission is to eliminate barriers and ensure that individuals from diverse backgrounds can access the extensive benefits of our national forests. This, combined with their portfolio of over three hundred existing visitor destinations – including six forest parks – positions them perfectly to embrace hutting.

Spanning forty-nine hectares, Carnock Wood was planted in 1950 with a variety of trees such as Scots pine, spruce, larch, Douglas fir and beech. It was selected as the pilot site for the inaugural hutting development on Scotland's national forest estate. The hutting village, encompassing four acres, is in the western section of the woodland.

These timber huts operate entirely off the grid, with no connections to mains water, electricity or sewerage. Heating is provided by wood stoves, water is brought in in containers using the communal wheelbarrow, and bottled gas is used for cooking. Composting toilets are to be installed at each hut.

At the time of writing in 2023, the first hut is complete – with others at various stages of construction – making this hutting community Scotland's current newest. If the project at Carnock Wood proves successful, it could pave the way for similar public land use models for hutting in the vast 8% of Scotland's total land, which is managed by Forestry and Land Scotland. The hutting future looks promising indeed!

LINDA

It was such a delight to visit Linda, the first Carnock wood hutter to have completed the build. She lives just a few miles from the site, but proudly declares that time at the hut has already changed her life for the better. Linda explained to me that when she was a young girl, her family had plans to move to a croft nestled in the countryside, but circumstances changed and that move sadly never materialised. By merit of building her hut, it's as though she's finally achieved that long-held childhood dream of embracing a blissful life amidst the beauty of nature, a calling that seems to be deeply ingrained in the very essence of human nature itself. As we sit chatting on her deck drinking hot tea from her stove, we watch two red squirrels dancing in the trees and Linda let out a joyful giggle that let me know her inner child was satisfied with her new hut life.

DES AND BEV, AND THEIR SON SEAN

This family were mid-build when I was at the woods; together, they were carrying the windows up to their hut frame, ready to be installed. I was very moved to see Sean helping his parents to carry materials and execute the jobs necessary to get the build done, as it reminded me of my own dad enlisting our help to build his hut. This cooperation, coordination and group effort really does help to ground a family and make the hut feel like it is truly theirs.

As we witness increasing numbers of huts appearing, the possibility of hutting becoming a part of the everyday lives of people in Scotland increases too. The visibility of huts builds awareness in a population that perhaps don't yet know that hutting might be for them, that it offers the chance to get out in the countryside and to really be part of it. The rise of the hut gives us reason to question that ubiquitous old phrase, "There is no place like home". Perhaps there is when you have a hut…

CHAPTER EIGHT

There's No Place Like Your Hytte

A h-uile latha sona dhut, gun latha idir dona dhut!

Every day good luck to thee, and no day of sorrow be!

Huts have a surprising ability to transform our experiences in alluring, enigmatic ways. An inherent power lies within the humble walls of a hut that grants us the freedom to simply be, without the pressure of constant, productive doing. Huts offer a place where we can consciously remove ourselves from the relentless demands and routines of our daily lives – which is arguably the best gift you can give yourself; the gift of "you time".

In the realm of huts, peace and quiet somehow hold a higher value, shaping the very fabric of the space. Here, interior design and decor choices play a significant role in cultivating an atmosphere conducive to tranquillity. Within the walls of a hut, we find the freedom to express ourselves in ways that may not align with the norms of a traditional house. The hut is a canvas for experimental and daring choices; an invitation to embrace shabby chic or kitsch aesthetics, to revel in high-tech marvels or the pared-back simplicity of minimalism. Whether you tend towards natural tones or vibrant pops of colour, the hut becomes a playground for the imagination, granting us the liberty to let our creative spirit roam free. How would your own hut look? Bear in mind you can do anything you like!

KAREN AND BRUCE'S HUT – FIFE

As I arrived at their hut to meet Karen, I couldn't help but be captivated by the understated elegance of its design. The hut has a modest interior, spanning just five by three metres – so it is considerably smaller than regulations allow, yet it provides just enough space to create a rarified retreat. A spacious deck terrace adorns the exterior, offering a seamless transition from the indoors to the outdoors, and neatly nestled beneath a small, slanted roof, is a wee covert kitchen stood ready among the trees to cater for the hutters.

"I keep the hut very minimalist, so that I am not looking around thinking, I should be doing this or that," Karen says. "I just keep my knitting here and try to stay off my phone." The kettle starts to sing on the stove and Karen pours the coffee. "It is a place to come to be quiet, peaceful and slow down," she muses, filling a flask with the excess boiled water; a classic hutter trick to keep it hot for later use.

Immersed in the hut's delightful aesthetics, I couldn't help but admire its rustic charm. Chunky exposed timber beams traversed the ceiling, adding a touch of natural beauty to the space. The walls were finished with textured plaster, which created a warm and inviting ambiance with its subtle pinkish hue.

A stylish light-coloured sofa bed stands as a focal point, inviting relaxation and contemplation. Next to it is a cabinet of shelves and otherwise there are only a select few items, carefully chosen for their sentimental value. "The milking stool was my mother's – she would use it when milking the goats – and that was the very first basket my friend Donald made." The items kept in the hut represent special memories of people or places dear to Karen and her husband Bruce – a clear reflection of the profound love and attachment they have already developed for their new hut.

The couple wanted a traditional-looking A-frame, so they modified the plans of the hut – making the pitch of the roof less steep, which gave them a higher back wall and the added benefit of extra headroom in the mezzanine sleeping area, as well as storage space in the eves. A lot of care has gone into the design, build and decor of this space and Karen explained to me that the orientation of the building was one of the biggest decisions they spent time deliberating over; their aim was to maximise the light at the plot.

"We brought a bench down to the bare site, and I would spend time watching how the light moved through the trees here. This helped us to decide where to place windows," she says with a smile.

"I painted all the windows myself – five coats!" she recalls. "They are all reclaimed. Building the hut dredged up old skills we hadn't employed for years, and we learned some new ones on the way." Karen became plaster apprentice to her friend Becky, who

is a master earth builder. Together they used local Fife clay mixed with some Cornish to get it just perfect; textured yet a wee bit rough and with that distinctive colour which gives a lovely warm feel to the hut's interior.

"We laid the floorboards ourselves; they were salvaged from a community centre in Dundee. The plan was to sand them, but once they were down, we enjoyed their character so much we kept them as they are." Karen's face lights up with the sense of achievement in having assisted in the build. I can see that this gives her not just ownership of the building, but has also centred her in it from the outset. She has a sense of belonging here.

Attention to the smallest details means the result is a serene space, with big windows looking onto the wooded surroundings. This design allows the couple to be comfortably

indoors and yet spot red squirrels, hares, tree creepers and even greater spotted woodpeckers all from the comfort of their hut.

All her life, Karen tells me, she has wanted to build a house, and the hut gave her the perfect opportunity to embrace that desire and even be bolder with the style decisions, freed of the practical constraints and demands of a more typical dwelling. In fact, she describes the hut as being, "A miniature version of my dream house!"

Karen's advice would be to not rush your hut build, go and experience the land fully before you start – and get a feel for the light. Think of where you want to have your morning coffee or take an afternoon snooze! Position your hut carefully to maximise your site and its light. In Scotland, you are likely to spend as much time in your hut as out, so be brave with your choices to create a space you will instantly love.

HUT HOBBIES

Every time we venture to our hut at Clachan Sound, I'm filled with a sense of amazement at how each trip holds its own unique charm, subtly distinct from the previous visits. While certain elements may remain familiar, such as chopping firewood, reading in my comfy chair and hoping that Coinneach will make those amazing fruit scones again, I've come to realise that the hut has evolved into a space where we almost instinctively embark on fresh adventures, defying the boundaries that ordinary life often imposes upon us.

Hobbies are sometimes associated with individuals leading quiet and relaxed lives. However, those of us with bustling, even stressful routines may benefit from hobbies even more. Engaging in pastimes brings forth numerous advantages that far outweigh the short bursts of time invested in them. Your hut serves as a sanctuary, granting you permission to pause amid your hectic schedule, allowing yourself to simply sit, unwind, and indulge in your favourite activities – whether that's wood carving, knitting Eriskay jumpers, learning Mòd songs, composing poetry or playing the guitar. The possibilities are endless, and your hut offers the ideal setting for embracing them.

Perhaps your hobby involves the art of cooking and experimenting with new recipes, or maybe you share Coinneach's passion for the joy of baking. Imagine the delight of combining activities, such as foraging fresh nettles to finally make that soup recipe you've been longing to try?

NETTLE SOUP

The Gaelic word *Feanndag* comes from the word *feannta* – to flay – as it blisters the skin. We've all been stung by a nettle and know that uncomfortable tingling feeling it can inflict. But cooked nettles can't sting you – and the nutritional value of this early green is well known in Scotland.

Nettles are coarse, upright perennials that are covered in those tiny wee stinging hairs. With their distinctive heart-shaped and tooth-edged leaves, the abundant nettle is very easy to identify!

Nettle (English common name)
Urtica diocia **(Latin)**
Feanndag (Scottish Gaelic)

When foraging your nettles – the best time is from February to June – use scissors and wear gloves for comfort. Select the young, tender new leaves. Or, on older plants, go for the top six leaves. By blanching the leaves, you remove the sting and can enjoy the spinach-like qualities of this plant which is rich in iron and vitamins A and C. Remarkably, nettles are also over 5% protein. This recipe serves four people.

TOP TIP! Why not try making nettle pesto? Don't worry, when crushed the leaves won't sting your mouth. If the idea appeals, see Trish's Vegan Wild Garlic Pesto recipe (on page 83), and substitute the wild garlic leaf for young nettles.

INGREDIENTS

- 2 onions
- 2 potatoes
- 1 leek
- 2 celery stalks
- 50g butter
- 200g tender nettle leaves
- 600ml chicken or vegetable stock
- Crème fraiche, to serve
- Grated nutmeg
- Salt and pepper, to season

METHOD

Put a pan of water on the stove and bring it to the boil. While that is heating up, you can sauté the chopped onion, leek, celery and potato in the butter for 10 minutes until soft and golden. Then liquidise, add the stock to the pan and heat it up.

Take the nettle leaves and plunge them in the boiling water for sixty seconds, then refresh under very cold water. Drain and then liquidise to a puree and add this to the pan. Don't cover the pan once you have added the nettle puree or the mixture will lose its colour. This brilliantly green soup is a spring booster, and it's a real shame to lose that fabulous verdancy!

Season well with salt, pepper and nutmeg and serve immediately with a dollop of crème fraiche in each bowl.

THE CRAFTY CABIN

The gratification that comes from conquering a challenge, or anything that causes us to enter that elusive "zone" and lose track of time, can be one of the building blocks of personal happiness. For me, that is playing with a blowtorch and metal. I know I am never going to be a jeweller, but the alchemy of molten metal becoming a wee trinket that I have bashed, sawn and soldered together brings me joy!

The tools I use to tinker at making things have a permanent home in a chest at the hut; I have a piercing saw, a bench peg, files, wee hammers and a blowtorch. We have a gas stove as a backup if the wood burner is not lit, which means there's always a gas cylinder there, making my hobby possible at the hut. I have been working on an owl scarf pin for my friend Eilidh for her birthday – she is very wise and also a hoot! Being at the hut gives me the permission I need to play at this pastime.

Similarly, whenever my friend Robyn comes to the hut, when not making toddies, she raids the art box and spends her time drawing – something she hadn't done since leaving school. The pleasure she finds in this is a reminder that we can always experiment with different hobbies and activities to uncover what truly brings us fulfilment and happiness. You might try a variety of different ideas to discover what you love and what works for you. And remember, just like me with my blowtorch, perfection isn't required…

ANDREW AND ELIZABETH'S HUT – FIFE

Andrew and Elizabeth co-designed their hut with Peter Caunt, and assembled a build team that included the talented Marrick, who is famed for his fine finish. Constructed with timber from local trees, a lot of thought went into the space. As Elizabeth is a wonderful cook, she created the outside kitchen, a feature which brings so much of their hut life outdoors. This design decision also allowed the interior to be more compact, which gives an intimate feel.

With a journey time of only thirty-five minutes by car from home to hut, they can make ultra swift mini visits, even popping down to their hut for an evening to have dinner on the deck before nipping back home!

Andrew's advice for would-be hutters is for them to create a new group, that way you bring people together and pull in the skill set which makes you stronger. He also recommends attending the Reforesting Scotland Annual Gathering to meet the hutting community. Andrew has found that they are always happy to share their experiences and expertise – and frequently people with land are in attendance, who might be able

to help with a suitable site. The Gathering – which is the very definition of "it takes a village" – is an annual event. Why don't you try to come along? Details are published early each year so check their website for the next date if you are interested.

For Andrew and Elizabeth, hutting brings a wonderful sense of well-being. Andrew feels truly fortunate that they found out about hutting via a chance encounter at one such Gathering. The rest is hut history! Their hut is just a few years old, but it has already positively enhanced their retirement in very fulfilling ways.

Countryside huts will most likely allow hutters a glimpse of nature that they might not otherwise enjoy. And part of that glimpse is slowing down and taking the time that affords us moments to enjoy life's little things, its incredible details. Or to get busy with the things that we don't usually have time to do . . . The benefits of hobbies, both psychologically and physically, are always worth exploring. Find something you enjoy engaging in – that provides just the right amount of challenge – and create time for yourself and your health.

HUTTER'S HACK
PINECONE BIRD FEEDER

During my visit to Karen's lovely hut in Fife, she showed me a charming and ingenious idea for nourishing our winged companions – the pinecone bird feeder. This heartwarming, straightforward hack requires nothing more than a pinecone and a piece of string. All you have to do is roll the cone in a generous layer of peanut butter and then sprinkle it with bird seed. Voilà! You've crafted a splendid, eco-friendly bird feeder, perfectly suited to attract feathered visitors to outside your hut.

THE BOTHY PROJECT

Initiated by artist Bobby Niven and architect Iain MacLeod in 2011, the Bothy Project is a unique and independent charitable organisation. Operating in a set of rural contexts, it provides residencies in bespoke small-scale, off-grid cabins – spaces to develop ideas, explore landscape and what it means to live simply.

The project's bothies provide accommodation and a place for imaginative working, inspired by Scotland's traditional mountain shelters. Collaborations with artists, designers and architects help develop each structure individually in response to its specific context.

SWEENEY'S BOTHY

Located in the Isle of Eigg on the west coast, Sweeney's Bothy was created in 2013 in collaboration with artist Alec Finlay. The contemporary mono-pitched structure perches on a hillside offering spectacular views across the sea to the nearby Isle of Rum. Check out the residencies programme and, who knows, perhaps there is a bothy stay ahead of you if you are an eligible creative soul.

The Bothy Project
www.bothyproject.com
Instagram @bothyproject

Now, the big question is, are you ready to make your own hut dreams a reality? If you are, then don't hold back. Go for it! As we shall now see, there are many different routes to becoming a hutter…

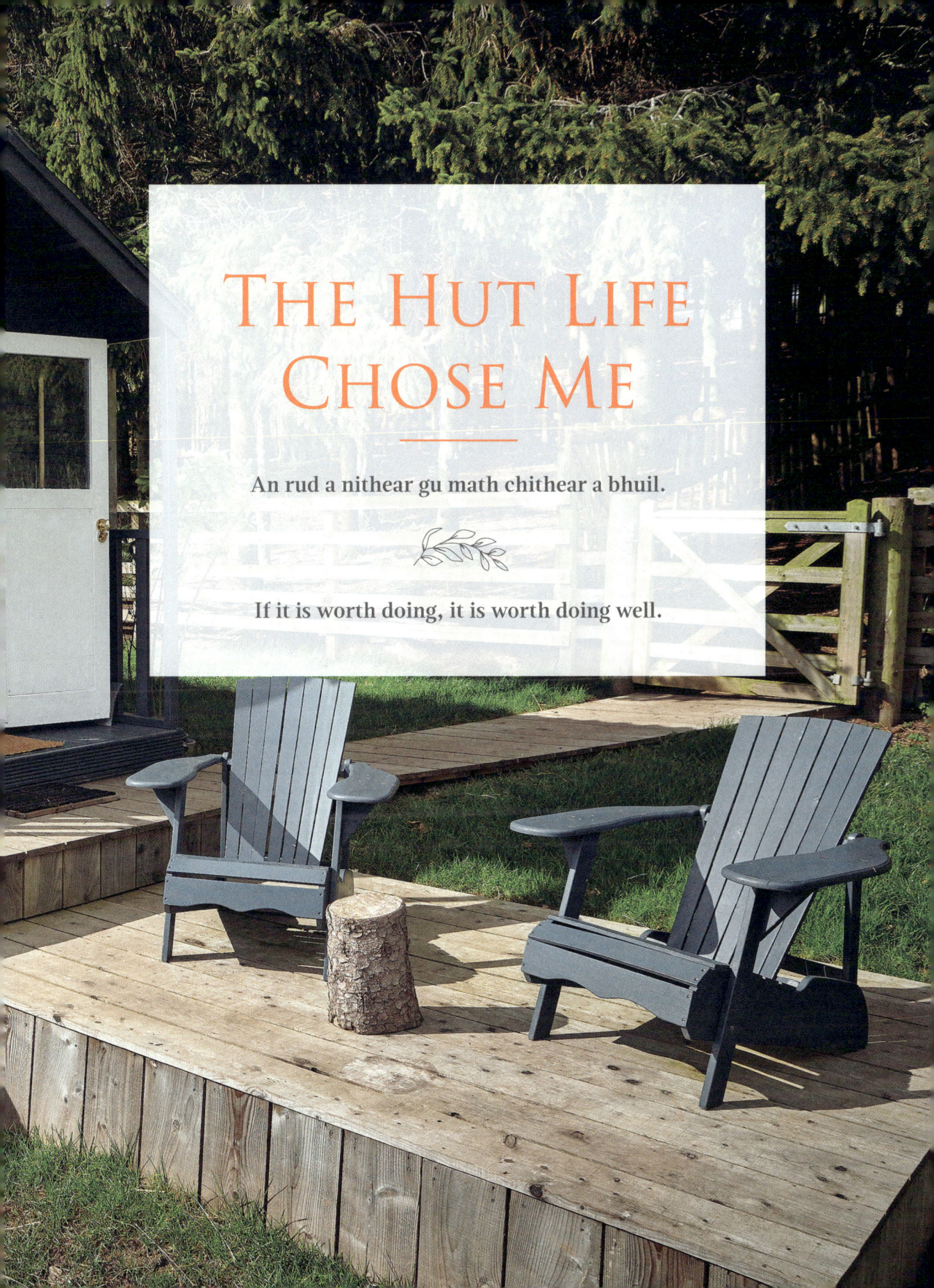

The Hut Life Chose Me

An rud a nithear gu math chithear a bhuil.

If it is worth doing, it is worth doing well.

So, are you ready for the good life? Let's look at the practical steps that you can take towards acquiring a site, building a hut and making this hutting dream of yours a reality. Let the hut life choose you...

Many individuals who choose the hutting lifestyle aspire to achieve a level of self-sufficiency through innovative and creative means. This motivation compels them to build their huts as protective havens against the elements: they devise methods to secure a water source for daily domestic needs, establish cooking facilities and ensure adequate heating and lighting within their wee cabins.

The locations where huts are typically situated often pose accessibility challenges, and hutting folk must also consider the ongoing need for storage space to accommodate wood, fuel and food supplies. Most people choose huts that are an easy commute from their home. The closer the proximity, the easier – and possibly more frequent – your short breaks will be. This crucial factor is worth bearing in mind when scouting locations.

Hutters tend to value reusing and preserving items that could potentially be useful in the future. This involves collecting various materials such as bits of wood, nails, screws, nuts and bolts, containers of all kinds, rope and string, pieces of pipe, and nearly any other salvageable material. The practice of keeping rather than discarding

items that may come in handy – especially since replacing them at a shop might not be immediately feasible – strikes me as a wise way to live!

This drive among hutters towards self-reliance impels many to seek to acquire knowledge relating to a myriad of subjects, including which herbs and plants to use for sustenance and medicinal purposes, skills in construction, rope usage, knot tying, fishing and foraging for food. Alongside their inventiveness is their desire to foster friendships and community – does this sound like you? If so, perhaps you are ready to take those next steps towards the creation of your own hut...

A BRIEF HUTTING CHECKLIST

Navigating the challenges of constructing a hut within the building regulations requires attention to detail and a dogged enthusiasm. As you start your hutting journey, it is important to consider the following:

- **SITUATION:** Where to build your hut? Think about proximity to home, access, drainage, possible water supply, the movement of natural light at a site...

- **HUT DESIGN:** Setting a budget and designing your bolt hole with an end goal in mind is important. This is your opportunity to create a space that works for you, your family and your friends.

- **THE BUILD:** Can you use recycled materials? What foundations, windows and insulation will you require?

- **SERVICES:** Without connecting to mains services, how will you make your hut as comfortable as possible? Think about solar power options, a composting toilet and access to water for washing and refreshments.

- **THE STOVE:** Fire is the heart of any hut, and your stove will give you heat, pleasure and cooking possibilities. Think about the practicalities. For example, where will you source fuel?

A THOUSAND HUTS FOR SCOTLAND

Through their Thousand Huts for Scotland Initiative, Reforesting Scotland have created an amazing and comprehensive resource on hutting; for example, they commissioned the Good Practice Guide to Hut Construction. This work eventually led to the definition of a hut being agreed in 2014, which in turn has facilitated planning permission applications. Later they were able to further influence the hut build criteria and the need for a building warrant in most instances was removed. These two important factors have stoked the fires and re-ignited interest in the hutting movement in Scotland by simply making the process easier.

For any prospective hutters, it is well worth exploring the pages of the website where you will find sound advice for your hut plans. A message forum on the site facilitates interactions within the hutting community. Who better to ask for advice than those who have already made their hut dreams a reality?

The goal is to help you build your hut successfully and safely – and within the existing rules and regulations. Here are six initial steps you could take on the path to building your hut.

www.thousandhuts.org

STEP 1 – CABIN STAYS

Stay in a hut and experience the lifestyle; that way, you will know if it is for you.

Scotland boasts some superlative commercial sector cabins, many of which are situated in stunning locations. You can decide if you'd like to be by a loch, in the hills, a forest or beside fields. They are also beacons of inspiration for what could be possible in a space you create for yourself. Here are some recommended cabins, but there are many more to be found online.

Inverlonan Bothies
www.inverlonan.com
Instagram @inverlonan

Ecotone Cabins
www.ecotonecabins.com
Instagram @ecotonecabins

Out of the Blue
www.outoftheblue.uk.com
Instagram @outoftheblueltd

Kabn Company
www.kabncompany.com
Instagram @kabncompany

Lochvenachar Cabins
www.lochvenacharcabins.co.uk
Instagram @loch_venachar_cabins

Monachyle Mhor
www.monachylemhor.net/stay
Instagram @themhorcollection

Guardswell Farm
www.guardswell.co.uk/stay
Instagram @guardswellfarm

Shepherd's Loch
www.shepherdsloch.com
Instagram @shepherds_loch

STEP 2 – HUT GOALS

Think about how you wish to make your hut happen. Are you a hermit hutter who hankers after solitude and peace? Or will you want to build within a community?

Regardless of whether you will build alone, or as a group, when searching for the perfect hut site in Scotland, several factors should be carefully considered. Our weather can be unpredictable; there is always the potential for experiencing four seasons in a single day. It is imperative that you construct a hut that can withstand the varying conditions, such as high winds or heavy snowfall.

The topography of a site plays a significant role in hut design. Whether situated on a hillside, moor, woodland or shoreline, the lay of the land will impact your hut's structure and foundations.

Working harmoniously with the site's existing nature will enhance your overall hutting experience. While trees can provide shelter from wind and rain, their presence may also affect the availability of natural light. Shoreline locations offer the advantage of being near water, but might require additional insulation. Hillside spots offer picturesque views, but necessitate tailored foundation structures based on the specific site characteristics.

Proximity to a water source is worth considering. A nearby loch or stream can serve as a convenient fresh water supply for a hut. Exploring clean water options can save the effort of transporting water via containers.

STEP 3 – FORM A GROUP

Consider finding or creating a group.

Find your tribe! This is a surefire way to reap the benefits of working with others towards making your hutting goals happen. There is power in the collective purchasing or leasing of land. This could make your hutting experience more affordable, and the journey may be more straightforward or more readily navigated as a group.

STEP 4 – FIND YOUR PLACE

Acquire a suitable site.

There is no right or wrong way to identify where your hut will ultimately be situated, but this is possibly going to be the most challenging decision of all. The distribution of land ownership in Scotland is very imbalanced, with a mere 0.02% of the population, equivalent to approximately 1,200 people, possessing two-thirds of the privately owned land.

As the hut movement grows, more landowners are awakening to the idea of having tenancy agreements with hutters, and thus new hut sites are springing up across the landscape. This means there are existing examples that can demonstrate how a new site could work.

Try approaching landowners with confidence and a clear proposal, as many may be open to leasing, or even selling land, especially if it offers a potential income stream in areas with limited prospects for generating revenue. For them, this may be an attractive option and some landowners genuinely wish to re-integrate people onto their land and thus create community benefits.

Demonstrating that you are easy to work with, respectful and that as hutters you will be good tenants and neighbours will increase the chances of a successful collaboration. Consult the Thousand Huts' Voluntary Code of Good Conduct Between Hutters and Landlords as a basis for discussing the many relevant issues before drawing up a lease.

Community or Forestry land may also be a feasible option for sites. The Carnock Wood project gives rise to a hopeful and bright future for huts located in collaboration with agencies that manage public land.

STEP 5 – RESEARCH & DESIGN

Embrace the experience of designing your hut. How are you going to make up to thirty square metres work for you?

In theory, this is the fun part! You get to design a space just for you, one that is tailored to your specific family situation. How do you want it to look? What is your desired outcome? What materials will you use? What can you re-purpose and recycle into your build? Let your imagination flow into this exhilarating world of possibilities – but bear in mind the current guidelines which define a hut. Chances are that you will only do this once, so make it count!

STEP 6 – COMMUNICATE WITH THE PLANNERS

Consult with your planning authority.

Remember, too, that you don't need to reinvent the wheel. Many planning authorities now have approved hutting projects. Look to see what has been approved in your council area; the drawings and reports can be found by searching their planning application portals. And, when communicating with planning officers, take your time and go back to basics if need be. You might need to explain the principles of hutting – don't expect every planning officer to understand your passion the way you do.

HUTTER'S HACK
HARNESSING THE POWER OF THE SUN

BASIC SOLAR TUTORIAL

Small-scale solar systems continue to improve in efficiency, reliability and affordability. They are perfect for huts as they are easy to fit, eco-friendly and can be a huge advantage for battery charging, lights and basic cooking.

A system consists of solar panels, an inverter/charger and battery storage. The panels can be sited on a south-facing roof or placed on the ground in a frame. This latter option is often best as it does not interfere with the roof and allows the panels to face directly south to maximise output.

The size of your system depends on the appliances you would want to use. Below are the approximate power requirement for different appliances; these can be used as a rough guide to estimate the size of system required.

A 3000-watt system would allow the use of any of these appliances, although not simultaneously. Appliances with lower power consumption may allow for a smaller system. Still, in Scotland, a backup generator will likely be required during the winter months and possibly even in summer if usage is high.

LED Lights (per lamp)	10 watts
Chargers	250 watts
Toaster	800 watts
Microwave	1500 watts
Kettle	2500 watts

BUILDING SMALL, LIVING LARGE

If you are not planning to self-build, you might consider hiring professionals for the design and building process. There are, of course, many builders out there who will be able to help you – but if this is the path you wish to take, then choosing a company that understands hutting will undoubtedly make the process smoother. Here are some recommendations.

NORTH WOODS DESIGN

Bespoke ecological timber huts and buildings, conscientiously crafted by a small family firm based in the Scottish Highlands. Bernard and his team always try to work on projects that can meet their own ethos and values – which includes hutting. They have worked on many cabin projects, and they find genuine reward in constructing quality structures.

www.northwoodsdesign.co.uk
Instagram @northwoodsdesign

QUERCUS RURAL BUILDING DESIGN

An architect-led design and build company that works in rural Scotland and is based in the Scottish Borders. Led by Peter Caunt – who is very knowledgeable about the hutting movement – they have an ecological and sustainable approach to builds that are healthy to live in, cheap to run and respect the planet's available resources. They can help you to assemble a team with the necessary skills for your hutting project. Specialising in the unusual, they are happy to tackle any type of construction challenges that other builders might shy away from.

www.quercusrbd.co.uk

BOTHY STORES

This social enterprise offers beautiful prefabricated modern cabin designs; their Bothy range features the Craft, Artist or Studio. Indeed, it is the Artist Bothy which appears on the front cover of *The Art of Hutting* – that particular wee beauty is situated at Inverlonan and is available for booking (see page 221). With a focus on slow living and reconnecting with life's fundamentals, these cabins are installed on site with a move-in turnkey service, which is ideal for enabling hutters to immerse themselves in activities that inspire them, in a place they love.

The emphasis is on fostering a relationship with nature through large windows and a gorgeous finish. Built with durable and sustainable materials inspired by vernacular architecture, these bothies come complete but can also be customised to your style and needs.

www.bothystores.com
Instagram @bothystores

GOOD WITH SPACE

Rob Moon is indeed very good with space and has form in the building of stunning cabins, huts, bothies and nature shelters. His client base appreciate thoughtful solutions and beautiful details. He is looking for intriguing briefs and loves to work with new hutters to measure-up, explore potential and come up with creative concepts that will deliver a build that exceeds expectations and will be enjoyed for years to come.

www.goodwithspace.com
Instagram @goodwithspace

Happy hutting!

Ruigidh each mall muileann.

A plodding horse will get to the mill.

By which we mean, you will get there in the end!

Whatever you do, please tag #theartofhutting if you are posting on Instagram. I'd love to follow along on your hutting adventures! Happy hutting, a chàirdean!

Just a wee deoch an dorais, just a wee drop, that's all.
Just a wee deoch an dorais, afore ye gang awa'
There's a wee wifie waitin' in a wee but 'n ben.
If you can say, "It's a braw bricht moonlicht nicht."
Then yer a'richt, ye ken!

Glossary of Gaelic terms

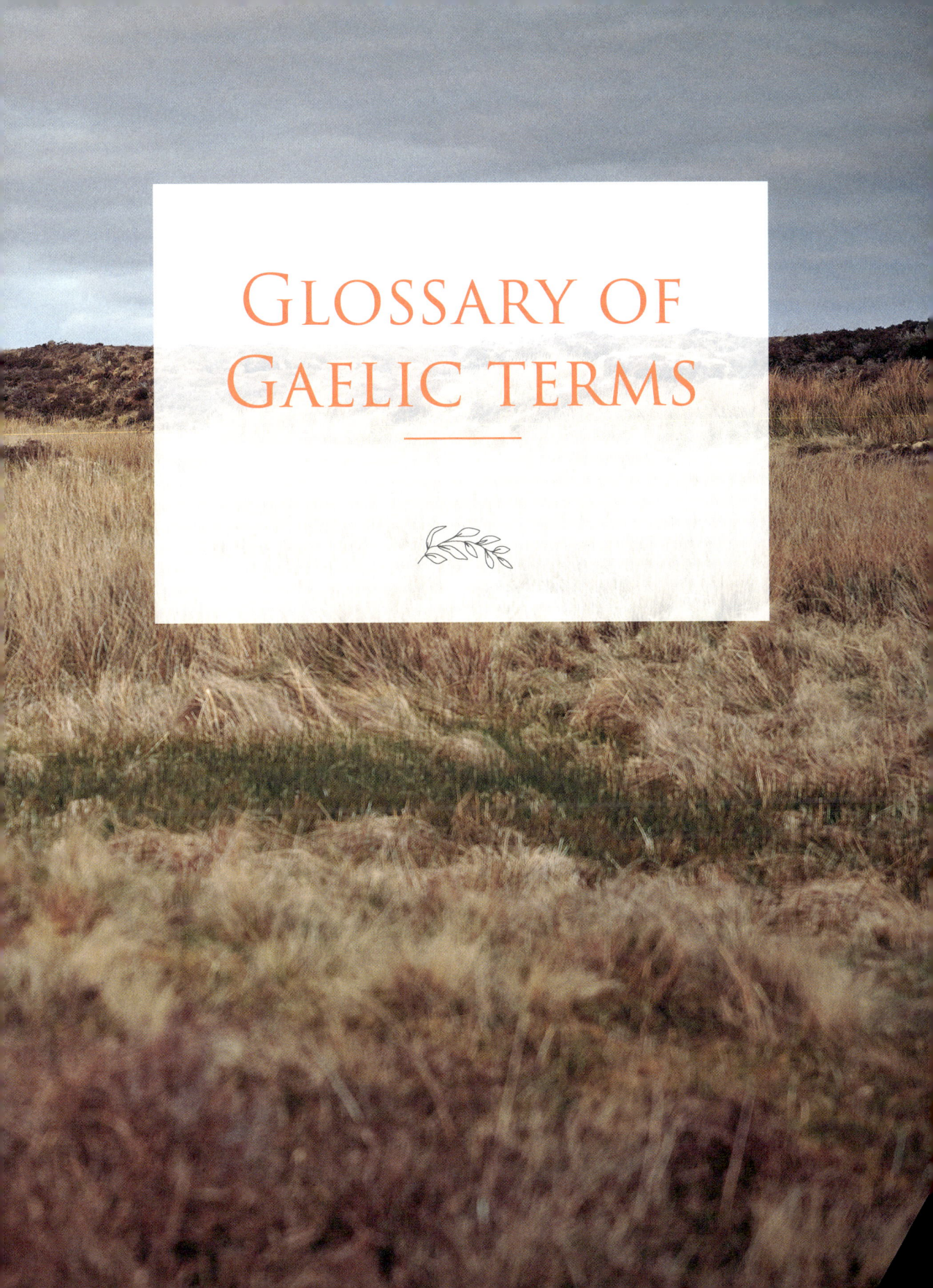

GAELIC	ENGLISH
Àirigh	Shieling
Àirighean	Shielings
Àirigh a' Bhealaich	Shieling on the brae
Alba	Scotland
Bàrd	Poet
Beith	Birch, Betula pendula
Bodach	Old man
Bothag	Hut
Bothan-àirigh	Shieling hut
Cailleach	Old woman
Calltainn	Hazel, Corylus avellana
Caorann	Rowan, Sorbus aucuparia
Cèilidh	Gathering, party, visit
Cleitean	Cleit; a stone storage hut uniquely found in St Kilda
Comhairle nan Eilean Siar	Western Isles Council
Copan	Cup (of tea)
Darach	Oak, Quercus robur
Deoch an dorais	One for the road, the last drink of the night
Droman	Elder
Duff	Clootie dumpling
Faidhbhile	Beech, Fagus sylvatica
Fàilte	Welcome
Fàilte a chàirdean	Welcome, friends

GAELIC	ENGLISH
Feanndag	Nettle, Urtica diocia
Gàidhealach	Highland
Gàrradh	Garden
Geansaidh	Jumper, jersey, sweater
Giuthas	Pine, Pinus sylvestris
Guga	Young gannet chick
Là Buidhe Bealtainn	May Day
Leòdhasach	A native of the Isle of Lewis
Na h-àirighean	The shielings
Niseach	Person from Ness
Mòd	Gathering, assembly, Gaelic cultural event of the year!
Seanair	Grandfather
Sgitheach	Hawthorn, Crataegus monogyna
Shen / Shennie	Abbreviated, affectionate form of the word seanair
Slàinte / Slàinte mhath / Slàinte mhòr	Good health, cheers
Taigh-cèilidh	Cèilidh house, social gathering place
Tairsgeir	Peat cutting iron
Tobar an Dualchais	Kist o Riches: online resource with recordings from across Scotland in English, Gaelic and Scots
Tobhtag	Small ruins
Uinnseann	Ash, Fraxinus excelsior
Uisge-beatha	Whisky: "water of life"

Throughout *The Art of Hutting* I have endeavoured to use a little Gaelic in a natural way – to give you a flavour of the language. If you are interested to learn more about Gaelic, then I recommend you look up **www.speakgaelic.scot**. This is a fantastic online learning resource and a great place to start your Gaelic learning journey.

MORE GAELIC LINKS TO EXPLORE

Sabhal Mòr Ostaig – Scotland's National Centre for Gaelic Language and Culture.
www.smo.uhi.ac.uk
Instagram @sabhalmorostaig

An Comunn Gàidhealach – Organisers of the annual Royal National Mòd.
www.ancomunn.co.uk
Instagram @royalnationalmod

Ceòlas – A community organisation based in Uist with a wide remit for language and traditional music development.
www.ceolas.co.uk
Instagram @ceolas_uibhist

Fèisean nan Gàidheal – An organisation that supports community-based Gaelic arts tuition festivals.
www.feisean.org
Instagram @fngaidheal

Duolingo – Features a Scottish Gaelic learning course, which is a fantastic – and free – access point for beginners.
www.duolingo.com
Instagram @duolingo

Am Faclair Beag – the most comprehensive Gaelic dictionary, and an amazing online resource.
www.faclair.com

Further to the amazing resources listed above, I also recommend that you tune in to the services of BBC Alba – which reflects the beating heart of Gaeldom today. The information and content that you will find on its website, television channel, socials and on Radio nan Gàidheal is unique and precious. In a world of media options, the range of refreshing programmes, amazing traditional and Celtic music, sport, drama, news, current affairs and entertainment is fantastic and the use of Scottish Gaelic in its natural form, in contemporary Scotland, offers a window to our lives, culture and heritage that you won't get anywhere else. It is the place for people who are interested in, or learning Gaelic to get a daily dose of the language!

A HUNDRED THOUSAND THANKS

Ceud Mìle Taing

I would like to thank my dad, my mum, Coinneach, my brothers Mark and Robin and of course Uncle Stuart for the precious times at the MacQueen family hut. As Granny used to say, "These ARE the good old days…" I'll see you all at the hut soon, I hope!

Massive thanks to Ali and Campbell and the entire team at Black & White Publishing (Simon, Emma, Tonje, Thomas, Hannah, Clem and Rachel), and Euan Anderson for touring Scotland with me and taking most of the braw photos that appear in *The Art of Hutting*.

My brilliant pals – who each contributed to this project in their own unique way – Chaya, Linda, Katrina, Greg and Sonny, Robyn, Julie, Ali and Roddy, Holly, Damo and Avery, Marion, Donna, Iain, Ann, Seumas, Jayne, Joy, Teàrlach and Maureen Flip. I love this rabble of characters dearly!

Extra special thanks to my lovely pal Faye – without whom the photos at the MacQueen hut would not have been possible.

Ceud mìle taing do Mhàiri Anna NicDhòmhnaill à Beàrnaraigh na Hearadh airson a còmhairle a thaobh na Gàidhlig.

I greatly appreciate the support of Alan Carter and Donald McPhillimy and their colleagues from Reforesting Scotland and the Thousand Huts initiative.

Thanks to the following people and locations for their support or for having us to visit: Carbeth Community, The Encampment, Games Loup, Old Torr Farm, Ninian Stuart, Hopeman, Carnock Wood, Findhorn, Eddleston huts, Richard Heggie, Chris and Lynn Jamieson at the Port na h-Eala fishing huts in Islay, Soonhope Huts, Glasgow City Council allotment sites at Kennyhill and New Victoria Gardens. Special thanks to Norman and Emily. In Lewis: Àirighean Chuidhsiadair agus Urras Oighreachd Ghabhsainn, Norse Mill and Kiln Society, Bosta Iron Age Round House, the Linda Norgrove Foundation, Grimersta Lodge, Uig Lodge and the Gearrannan Blackhouse village.

If you are looking for a new hobby, I recommend contacting the amazing Antje from The Yarn Cake in Partick, Glasgow – www.theyarncake.co.uk – and the wonderful Scott from Vanilla Ink Studios in Glasgow where you can learn jewellery-making skills – www.vanillainkstudios.co.uk. Thank you to both these creative businesses for supporting this project, and for your friendship over the years.

Last, but certainly not least, huge thanks to all the hutters, beach hutties, cabin folk and shieling holders from across Scotland who welcomed me on my *The Art of Hutting* travels into their worlds. It was a joy and a privilege to meet you all and to visit each of your unique wee huts.